Small Space Gardens

David Stevens

Small Space Gardens

HDi

HARPER
DESIGN
international

An imprint of HarperCollinsPublishers

Being married to a workaholic is not easy and so much

thanks are owing to my wife Pauline.

SMALL SPACE GARDENS

Text © David Stevens 2003
Design and layout © Conran Octopus 2003
Illustration © Conran Octopus 2003

Publishing Director: Lorraine Dickey
Senior Editor: Muna Reyal
Managing Editor: Gillian Haslam
Copy Editor: Sharon Amos

Creative Director: Leslie Harrington
Art Editor: Alison Fenton
Picture Research: Mel Watson
Illustrator: Russell Bell

Production Manager: Angela Couchman

First published in the United States in 2003
by Harper Design International
An imprint of HarperCollins*Publishers*
10 East 53rd Street, New York, NY 10022

First published in the United Kingdom in 2003
by Conran Octopus Limited
A part of Octopus Publishing Group
2–4 Heron Quays, London E14 4JP

First Edition
Printed and bound in China
1 2 3 4 5 6 7 / 09 08 07 06 05 04 03

Library of Congress Cataloging-in-Publication Data

Stevens, David, 1943-
    Small space gardens / David Stevens-- 1st ed.
       p. cm
    ISBN 0-06-056760-0 (hc)
    1. Landscape gardening. 2. Gardens--Design. I. Title.
SB473.S8432 2003
712'.6--dc21   2003047892

CONTENTS

Introduction

A garden, however small, is a blessing. A green oasis in the heart of town, a country courtyard, a roof terrace perched high above the city – all have their own charm, purpose and unique character. The sad fact, of course, is that many such places do not realize this potential, ending up as an awkward afterthought, poorly planned and poorly planted, of little use to their owners or the house they adjoin. In reality even the most uncompromising yard has potential, the secret is to see, understand and make the best of it. A challenge, maybe, but the end result can be more than worth the effort, providing an outside room that fits you and your family like a glove.

The problem so often is while we are comfortable planning rooms inside the home, more often than not we lose our way outside. Gardens, however small, are never the quick fix many television makeover programmes would have us believe; they develop, grow and mature. They are a subtle blend of paving, walling and structures interlaced and overlaid with plants that breathe life into the composition. The style of the garden is up to you. It may be a contemporary extension of the most modern architecture or a soft, sensual and sinuous place winding between narrow boundaries. It may be formal or raspingly deconstructivist. None of these is right or wrong, simply different – you can plan a garden a thousand different ways. Nor should we take ourselves too seriously; gardens should be joyous places. Naturally, the smaller the space, the more critical the planning, but your yard can so easily be multi-functional with room for play, relaxation, cooking, dining and the opportunity to grow anything from herbs to broad-leafed exotics. Minimalism can play its part, too, and a garden that contains purity of line and the utmost simplicity can be a place of great beauty.

In all of this it is clear that any garden needs a game plan – a successful yard does not simply happen. Design is the starting point, with the analysis and creative ability not only to organize the garden to accept what you want within the boundaries but also to absorb and embrace what lies beyond. I have been designing gardens for over thirty years with pleasure, frustration, hard work and not a little success. As a professional I know how important sequential planning is and how much easier it is to take things a step at a time. Small gardens are an enduring passion of mine. As well as owning several, I cut my design teeth on them when studying landscape architecture in London at the start of my career. These often awkward, little places hold endless fascination and when you get them right, enormous satisfaction. In this book I will take you through the whole design process, demystify it and pass on some invaluable tricks of the trade.

As a final thought, it is worth remembering that our garden is just that. This is not a place for fashion that quickly palls, but somewhere to exercise our imagination, needs and passions. Most things in this world are designed for us, a garden thankfully is not and offers an endlessly fascinating canvas on which to paint an equally fascinating composition – enjoy!

Left You should enjoy the spaces outside in equal proportion to those inside your home. Simplicity is often the key and in this tiny court there is a delicate blend of materials to link with the adjoining house.

ANALYSING YOUR SPACE

1

Assessing your needs

The best gardens, however large or small, have a feeling of rightness. They are comfortable places without clichés; they rarely pander to fashion nor are they too neat, pristine or overcomplicated. As a garden designer I visit many homes and, as soon as I walk through the door, I can tell just what kind of people I am going to meet and what their preferences are likely to be. The clues are all around – in the colour schemes, furnishings, ornaments and general ambience of the home environment. From my point of view, I have to assimilate all this pretty quickly, but when you are planning your own space you have time on your side.

The real point behind this is that any form of design is an analytical process and the more thorough the analysis, the better the end result. Like anything worthwhile, gardens don't just happen. They are moulded and modified by a whole range of circumstances: the shape and size of the plot, the orientation, the views, the type of soil, situation and, most importantly, *your* personality.

In all probability, you bought your house or apartment because you liked it. There was something about the layout and size of the rooms, the style of architecture and the location that appealed to you – very often the garden, too, forms part of this decision-making process. The choice of where and how you live was a positive one. Almost certainly, however, you will want to change things, both inside and out. More often than not, it's the house that needs your attention first, but don't – and this is vital – ignore the garden during this all-important planning stage. If you glean just one thing from reading this book, it should be the fact that inside and outside living are inseparable. If you treat them as such you are well on the way to achieving spatial harmony, which is the basis of all good design.

Left With a brand new home you may have a completely clean canvas with which to create a garden. However, it will still be important to check out everything inside and outside the boundaries. Here you can see that the neighbouring house has been screened with hedging and the awkward angle of the fence on the other side of the garden plays host to a pool and planting. The Pennisetums provide a visual link across the space while the floor is given over to a neat combination of pre-cast slabs and cobbles.

Opposite Whatever the state of your garden you need to check just what is there in terms of trees, planting, changes in level and, of course, boundaries. These could be fences, walls or hedges and be in good or bad repair. For an unexpected, radical touch, you could turn this crumbling wing into an artwork.

Taking this principle a little further, it is natural that you check out the sizes and proportions of the rooms inside: after all, you would not order a carpet or a suite of furniture without knowing the overall dimensions. It is also true that you are unlikely to mix different styles in the same room and will almost certainly choose a particular theme, which may also extend to other parts of the house. Similarly, you should not think of exterior planning without a basic fact-finding process that will allow you to allocate space and choose a style effectively.

Many years ago I ran a postal garden planning service for a national magazine and to do this effectively I had to devise a simple method to help customers gather the information I needed. This came down to just two basic questions: what have you got? and what do you want? Both require a degree of practical analysis and, at the end of the day, practicality figures high in the preparation of any successful design.

The creation of a garden should never be a quick fix and this applies equally well to the delicate process of absorbing everything that will impinge upon or shape the composition to come. There should never be any great hurry, particularly in a garden you have just moved into, and there is a good deal of sense in taking your time to gather the information you need – over the course of a full year is ideal.

Seasonal changes

In many parts of the world there is a definite turning of the seasons, each bringing its own particular beauty in terms of the strength of light, temperature and growth of plants. In temperate climates late winter and spring will see bulbs bursting into life to herald the new year; buds open, new foliage shimmers and the garden shakes itself free of long, cold nights. Hardy perennials hitherto unnoticed take their place in borders, blossom unfolds and, as summer approaches, the garden swells to its full proportions. Autumn brings colour and late bloom; even in the smallest yard fruit and vegetables are ready to harvest as the season draws to a close. Then the cold days of winter approach, when the garden revels in its sparse beauty. In other regions the climate may be significantly different or there may not be such a marked difference in the seasons, but in every case it will play a vital part in just how you live outside.

Left The internal garden layout often takes its cue from the house and here the warm terracotta-coloured walls are carried over to the solid bench seats and table. Built-in furniture can save a huge amount of space in a small garden and become a part of the overall composition. The Italian cypress adds a dash of verticality while the sculptures provide a personal touch.

Many people take all this for granted, but by taking time out to really study your garden for a year you start to get inside the presence of the thing – its moods, good points, limitations and character. As the year turns you will see that the sun pitches higher or lower in the sky, in turn casting longer or shorter shadows. This will largely determine not just where you will sit, dine or entertain but also what will grow in your garden. Plants are site specific, and I'll talk more of that later, but there are species for every situation – even the shadiest basement plot can be swathed with foliage to soften unyielding walls.

Views

In a small garden you need to think about maximizing the space at your disposal. While the area will naturally have physical limitations, don't forget the potential of what may lie outside the plot.

Just occasionally the views may be stunning: a distant glimpse of the sea, a rolling landscape, a flurry of vernacular pitched roofs or a fine tree in a neighbour's garden. Some of these things may not be immediately obvious. I will always remember the time a client told me they had a wonderful view from a first-floor window. Indeed they had: the sea was perfectly framed by a tree in their own relatively small garden and an adjoining house. As a result we built a tree house, which had the effect of not only embracing the view but also freeing up valuable space at a lower level. Look at your own yard and its views from as many places as you can – you may be pleasantly surprised. Catching such a view is called borrowed landscape and is one of the most important elements in making a small garden seem bigger.

On a slightly more mundane, but nevertheless important, level, you may well have the opportunity of linking your garden visually to your neighbour's. There might be a group of shrubs cascading over your boundary or a particular species of tree. How much more pleasant if you can join those plantings together, screening your boundary in the process so that you don't quite know where one garden ends and the other begins. There are many ways to handle tiny outside spaces, but one of the best is to cocoon yourself in greenery, which can often take its cue from what lies beyond. It may well be just an illusion but that illusion is well worth having.

Conversely, views can easily work the other way around and in many a garden a bad aspect is only too obvious. However, all but the worst can usually be screened, perhaps with a judiciously placed small tree, a higher fence, or

Below Just occasionally views are sent from heaven and to ignore them would be a sin beyond redemption. However, a wall can mask all kinds of low-level nasties and allow a distant view, in this case the mountains, to draw the eye in all its glory. The Bougainvillaea provides continuity while a gloriously simple water feature provides interest within the garden.

Above In reality there are many more bad views than good and, in this case, a solid boundary made from corrugated metal sheeting, provides the necessary screening. Minimalist-style gardens and architecture call for minimalist boundaries and there is a cleanliness of line in the galvanized fence that is echoed by the trough and metal grid paving.

Right Just a glimpse of a view can often be more telling than a wide open vista and here the distant meadow definitely invites you to take a closer look. The arched hedge helps to emphasize a feeling of tension and the foreground grasses are a clever link with the crops in the field.

overheads that run out from the house over a sitting area, to screen it from neighbouring windows at a higher level that look directly into the garden.

Not all neighbours or situations are ideal: there may be a busy road or school close by or loud people next door. Space permitting, heavy planting can do a good deal to soak up noise, while positioning a water feature by a sitting area can work wonders. I built a garden for a client living close to a major airport and used a water wall, which was both dramatic and a real focal point, to literally block out the noise of aircraft passing overhead. Substitution is a great design tool, both in terms of one noise masking another or encouraging a view away from a particular area towards a better one.

At this stage I am not suggesting that you get too specific; there will be time to plan the garden in detail later. What is necessary during this initial fact-finding is to get a feel of what your garden is all about. Most people, and students learning design for that matter, make hard-and-fast decisions too soon. It is also true that design by committee – and in a domestic situation that means the family – is often far more productive than input by one person alone. Remember that this space will be used by everyone – children and animals too – and all need to be catered for.

Creating a wish list

While gathering information you will also be getting all sorts of ideas on what you want to see in the garden. Designers have a simple checklist of all the possible features that can be incorporated in any composition. We run through this with our customers and make a note of all their preferences. At this stage, it helps to think about what you want in general terms and if you start making a list this can be refined later on.

Up to now I have been talking a lot about practicality, for the simple fact that good design is much to do with just that. But what most people, and designers too, really want to get into is creativity – and this is a vital part of your wish list. While you were gathering all that information you were naturally thinking about what you wanted. You have probably been ripping pages out of magazines, gathering catalogues from suppliers and visiting garden centres or shows. Try getting a big noticeboard and pinning up the images so that you can see them from day to day without delving into a file. Change them around, take photographs of other gardens, decide what you *really* like, what turns you on. Gardening is a sensual, even a sexy business, and romance can figure highly, even with all the practicality. Imagery is therefore vitally important, but don't get seduced by silly fashion – that's something else entirely, shallow and transient.

It is also worth bearing in mind that any outside space may well have to incorporate the practical, or even ugly, as well as the handsome. Rubbish bins, washing lines, a shed, store or other utility items are often component parts. There's no point in ignoring these: if considered at the planning stage, they can often be cleverly worked in and disguised. A flat-topped bin store can have room to house a display of pot plants on top. A washing line can neatly recoil into a wall mounting and an essential shed can be painted up, linked into overhead beams or trellising and become a very positive element in the design. In other words, practical elements sensitively handled can become part of the overall garden composition.

By now you will be starting to get a feel of the way the space works. You probably enter by a specific doorway that is angled in a particular direction. This in turns leads to a view – in design terms called an axis. This may be a good aspect, or simply face the back of someone's garage: either way it will need dealing with. You will have noted just where the sun swings throughout the day and the shadow patterns created by boundaries, trees and adjoining buildings. This in turn will suggest where you may sit, either in a sunny or shady spot. In most areas there will also be a prevailing wind and although in an urban garden this will be deflected by surrounding buildings, it will still blow from a particular direction for much of the year. There may be a chill draught that whistles around the corner of the house or, in a kinder climate, a particular place that catches a cool breeze during the hottest part of the day. From one you may need protection while the other will determine where you can enjoy its full effect.

From all of this you will see that a pattern is starting to emerge and, while the garden layout is not yet finalized, you are well on the way to setting the main parameters. The characteristics of the site are starting to drive the design and not, as so often happens, the other way about. So many gardens are created as fashion statements and, as a result, turn their back on all kinds of inherent advantages. If you work with an environment instead of against it, you have the opportunity to create something very sympathetic, as well as special. This, again, is something that all good gardens have in abundance and it boils down to that indefinable feeling of rightness you experience as soon as you enter the space.

But we haven't finished checking things out yet and there are a number of other factors that could make a big difference to the final planning stage. Many a garden, even the smallest yard, may have quite severe changes in level (see pages 66–67). Look on these as a real bonus: they can create drama and potential in ways that a flat plot never can. The down side is the budget, which I'll talk about on page 28. Retaining walls, steps and other split-level features can cost a reasonable amount of hard-earned cash, which makes potential design even more important – you only want to carry out such work once.

Above Just what kind of garden you own is directly related to your personality and wish list. It may be crisp and cool, unashamedly laid back or as shown here, an urban jungle. This composition has character by the spadeful as well as division into separate areas. The pink wall offers a home to climbing plants as well as tempting you to explore the area beyond while the lush sub-tropical planting sets up a wonderful dialogue of different shapes, forms and textures.

Up to now I have been primarily interested in the spatial potential of the garden and have said little about planting, apart from borrowed landscape or screening. In a garden the planting will help bring the space alive with colour and interest throughout the year. When you move into a new house, you may inherit anything from an overgrown jungle to a virgin plot, so this is the time to take a considered look at what you will keep and what has to go. The problem very often is a natural reluctance to remove well-grown specimens, even though these may be growing in the wrong place. This is a time for reflection and weighing up just what potential a group of shrubs or a tree may have.

Using existing planting

What is wrong – and potentially disastrous – is to go out with a 'slash and burn' policy that denudes the area of any vegetation at all. It may seem attractive to start with a completely clean canvas but remember it takes five minutes to take a tree down with a chainsaw yet many years for it to grow. I can't remember how many times I have visited gardens where the new owners have suggested this course of action, when in fact the existing planting, although unsightly, really did have potential when examined in detail.

In one instance, a small garden that had once been part of a far larger plot had a straggling line of old espaliered fruit trees running most of the way across, at a particularly awkward angle. These had grown into Arthur Rackham-esque shapes: outstretched branches clutched at one another while the trunks were gnarled with age. The clients, understandably, were not keen to retain these ancient and non-productive specimens but there was something undeniably exciting and sculptural in their outline. After a good deal of talking, I persuaded them to leave them, at least for the time being, to see if there was something positive that could be achieved by their survival. This was to be a modern garden, no holds barred, and after plotting everything out and getting the details on the drawing board, a pattern started to emerge. The odd angle of the espaliers suggested the entire garden layout. To one side they thrust their way into a deck, on the other side a raised bed in stainless steel reversed the angle, jutting dynamically towards the house. Glass beads and pools of water swirled around and through the trees while new stainless steel wires and bottle screws were threaded between the old limbs to add support and purity of line. The final result was a vibrant, exciting garden, the old trees acting as a divider, feature and even provider of fruit once pruned correctly. Here was a perfect example of ancient and modern working together in harmony, but who would have thought of it at first glance.

Conversely, it could have turned out that these trees had no potential at all, in which case they would have been removed to allow the design free rein. The point is simply to remind you to keep an open mind in these initial design musings; nothing is set in stone at this stage, nor should it be. It is much

Left Mature trees, providing they are a suitable species and in the right place, can be a real bonus in a small garden. Often they can form a pivot or major focal point within the design as well as a rich habitat for wild life and a natural windbreak. The shade cast by overhanging branches can be a godsend on a hot summer's day. In this garden an elegant and beautifully detailed deck constructed around the base of the tree trunk is backed by a screen wall that offers division from the rest of the composition.

easier to change your mind now than when the garden is constructed. Thoughts, pen and paper are cheap; permanent or semi-permanent planting has far-reaching consequences.

Existing planting may have other advantages. Shelter and screening from a bad view should be pretty obvious but don't underestimate the ability of a dense shrubbery or group of trees to filter the effects of a strong wind. This is a natural part of your survey and fact-finding process. A prevailing wind may not always be apparent so check your garden on a regular basis to pick up on this kind of outside influence. Again, the existing planting may look uncompromising but perhaps with some thinning and replanting the area can be improved, while still retaining its screening potential.

One or more trees will also cast shade and this might be particularly useful when thinking about the position of a seat or sitting area. Trees also take water and nutrients from the soil as well as influencing what species will grow beneath them.

We are constantly being exhorted by worthy environmentalists to preserve wildlife. But in a small garden piles of rotting logs or bramble and nettle patches are neither *de rigueur* or practical. However, an existing water feature could well be renovated to good advantage and mature planting will provide a habitat for all kinds of beneficial creatures. Indigenous species are particularly useful in this respect and this is another reason for identifying existing plants if you can. Any garden has the potential to be a balanced environment and a mix of features will help achieve this.

Checking the soil

While thinking of planting in these basic terms we also need to check what kind of soil we have. So many people ignore this vital constituent, which is after all, the growing medium for all plants. Many of the latter are quite choosy about what they will tolerate. Some enjoy acid conditions, others an alkaline or chalky soil and if you buy a plant from a good garden centre or nursery it should state this on the label. Don't expect acid lovers to grow on chalk or vice versa. There are many easy-to-use soil testing kits available that will allow you to check conditions in several parts of the garden.

Soils may be heavy or light and I can't recall how many times desperate gardeners have asked me how to improve the former. In fact, heavy clays can be remarkably fertile as the constituent grains are small and therefore tend to hold nutrition far better than a sandy soil. The problem is that they warm very slowly and are the very devil to cultivate. However, the addition of organic material such as compost or well-rotted manure will be enormously beneficial, helping to break down a heavy soil and bind together something altogether lighter. This is known as 'soil conditioning'.

In cases where a garden is waterlogged or very damp, you may have to consider laying drains of some kind, although deep cultivation may improve things enormously. Drainage is often best left to a specialist contractor and it may be well worthwhile calling on their expertise in such situations.

Right This is a perfect 'come hither' composition, the broad and generous brick path, laid in a 'basket weave' pattern leading the eye towards the delightfully soft grass and chairs surrounded by background planting. The important thing here is that there is nothing contrived, just good sense and that is very much what comfortable gardens are all about.

Carrying out a survey

By now you may well have the basis of a garden design developing in your mind. You will have absorbed the charisma of the place, its good and bad features, the entry points, the architecture of the adjoining house, the passage of the sun and much else. Of course there will still be a good deal of detail to think about but, by resisting the temptation to jump in and build or even draw the garden immediately, you will start to visualize things three dimensionally, which is just what professional designers are taught to do.

With the initial homework done and the basic facts gleaned, we need to start refining our thoughts into a realistic working plan that will bring the garden alive. While the broad picture we have developed is excellent in theory and allows us an insight of the garden to come, practicality linked to attention to detail will really bring the design to fruition. To achieve this we need to look at everything in rather more detail and make a basic survey so that we can draw a plan of the garden to scale. It is at this point that many people wonder why this is necessary. Why can't we simply sketch the design roughly on a piece of paper or peg it out loosely on the ground and then get on with construction immediately? Some rare people can do this and create the most stunning compositions, but they are usually gifted individuals with a innate eye for space, shape and form that allows them to visualize the garden to come. For most people this is not a realistic option and the advantage is that a drawing

Left However natural a garden may look once established, remember that all of this needed planning, which in turn depended on an accurate survey. Here lushly planted beds have been shaped to draw the eye up the slope towards the pots and sitting area that act as a focal point. The trellis allows a glimpse of something beyond, a simple trick to increase a feeling of space.

and subsequent design drawn to scale is *accurate*. You can work out proportions, allocate space, calculate the quantities of materials that you need, prepare a planting plan and, in the long run, save yourself a great deal of time, money and effort.

Carrying out a garden survey is both straightforward and fun, reinforcing much of your initial thinking. Start by drawing the approximate outline of the garden on a sheet of paper. Do this outside and use a clipboard. Draw in the outline of the house and mark clearly the position of doors and windows. These will be vital and may well determine the design axis or focus on a particular view within or even outside the garden. Mark in the boundaries and make a note of what they are made of – fence, hedge, wall or perhaps the side of an adjoining property. Check their height, condition, and if they are painted any particular colour. Now mark in any existing paved areas, again noting the materials – brick, pre-cast concrete slabs, decking or any one of many surfaces. It may be that you already know such an area will not fit comfortably into your new scheme. If this is the case, don't waste your time plotting it accurately but make a note of the materials involved – you may be able to lift these and re-use them elsewhere. The position of any drains or manholes is particularly important. These are often close to the house and set at an awkward angle. There are ways around the problem, like using recessed covers or turning them to match a particular paving pattern. The important thing is never to cover them over: one day you may need to find them in a hurry.

If there is a slope or steps, indicate these on your plan and measure the drop involved. The latter may well determine how different levels in the garden are created, together with all kinds of features including pools, raised beds, terracing and much else.

Now is the time to mark in the position of those good or bad views. Do the same for the direction of a prevailing wind and don't forget that all-important north point that indicates where the sun will be at mid-day. It may be easier to indicate where the sun rises and then draw an arc across the drawing to the position of sunset. In this way you can work out where the sun is at any particular time, which is useful for positioning a sitting area, seat, herb plot and plenty of other things. If you checked the soil in different parts of the garden and there was a marked difference in acidity or alkalinity, note the sample positions.

Now mark in any existing plants, but only those that you know are worth keeping. Try to identify them so that you can determine their eventual size and their relationship to any new species you introduce. Remembering the borrowed landscape principle, note any shrubs or trees growing in your neighbour's garden. Draw in the outline of the canopy if it extends over your space. It will naturally cast shade and provide a ceiling that could have all kinds of positive implications.

Garden trees are particularly important: a young sapling that may look just right when you move in could grow into a monster that dominates the garden and threatens drains, buildings and becomes a pest. It will be far easier to take it out now rather than ten or fifteen years on, when you may need to hire an expensive tree surgeon with specialist equipment. In a small garden forest species are usually unsuitable – don't be seduced into keeping them just because they look inoffensive when young. A degree of subjectivity is an important aspect of any planning work, particularly when you are dealing with living and developing plant material. Trees and high hedges, especially the coniferous kind, cause more disputes between neighbours than anything else in the garden. If you have a problem in this respect, do try to solve it in a diplomatic way. Remedial action may well suit both parties and an independent comment from a tree specialist can smooth the way. Incidentally, conifer hedges can be an excellent screen and help to soak up noise. The secret is in clipping them from an early age, with the top slightly narrower than the bottom. Feed and water regularly, as they are gross feeders and tend to impoverish the surrounding soil.

Taking measurements

Now comes the job of measuring everything, but don't panic, it is simple! Over the years I have measured hundreds of gardens, mostly by myself with a tape measure. If a garden is very complicated, with changes of level, awkward slopes at different angles, trees and anything else, get a professional surveyor to do the job – the fee will be well worth it. In a small garden, however, this is rarely necessary. Buy or borrow a long tape measure (dressmaker's tapes or short steel tapes are not long enough to do a proper job, although the latter may well be useful for checking awkward corners or details). I always use running measurements (see page 25). I anchor the tape to one boundary and run it out along the face of the house. I leave it unreeled on the ground, making sure it is taut, and then go back to the beginning and note the measurements down in sequence. Everything is checked off: the position of a path or terrace, the edge of the building, windows, doors, drains, manholes and so on – right across to the far boundary. Then I repeat the exercise at right angles, down the garden, picking up details such as paving, planting and positions of any trees (as well as indicating the position of the trunk, note the spread of the canopy too).

In many old town gardens the boundaries are not square, with one or more running off at an angle. To check these you need to follow a simple measuring technique known as triangulation, which will positively fix the corners in position (see page 25). To do this you need to measure from two known points – I often use the two ends of the house. Run a tape from one end of the house to the corner of the garden and make a note of the distance. Then move the tape and measure the distance from the other end of the house. When you prepare the scale drawing (see page 27), you extend a pair of compasses to the correct distance and draw an arc for each of the measurements. Where the two arcs intersect is the exact position of the corner of the garden. This technique works well for trees or any other feature that you cannot easily measure using running measurements.

You will be surprised at all the details the survey reveals and how these have potential in the design you create. You will now have all the information and measurements you need to create a drawing of your garden to scale.

SURVEY OF THE GARDEN

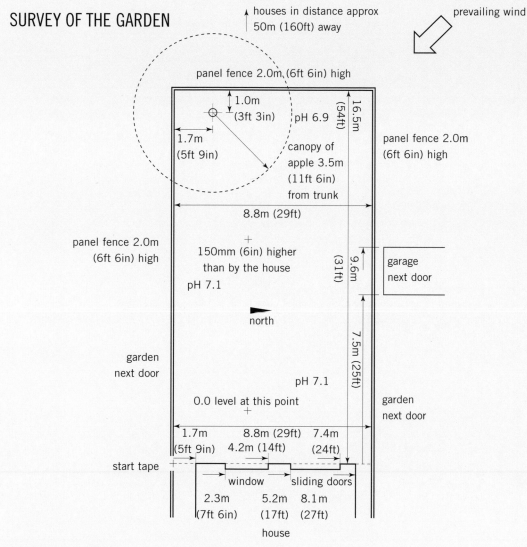

houses in distance approx 50m (160ft) away

prevailing wind

panel fence 2.0m (6ft 6in) high

1.0m (3ft 3in)

pH 6.9

16.5m (54ft)

panel fence 2.0m (6ft 6in) high

1.7m (5ft 9in)

canopy of apple 3.5m (11ft 6in) from trunk

8.8m (29ft)

panel fence 2.0m (6ft 6in) high

150mm (6in) higher than by the house
pH 7.1

9.6m (31ft)

garage next door

north

7.5m (25ft)

garden next door

pH 7.1

garden next door

0.0 level at this point

1.7m (5ft 9in)

8.8m (29ft)
4.2m (14ft)

7.4m (24ft)

start tape

window

sliding doors

2.3m (7ft 6in)

5.2m (17ft)

8.1m (27ft)

house

Left On this simple survey all the information that you will need to prepare a scale drawing is clearly shown. You can see that the tape has been fixed on the left hand fence and then unreeled across the garden to obtain 'running' measurements along the back of the house. Levels are clearly shown together with the apple tree and, most importantly, the extent of its canopy. The bad view of houses as well as the garage next door are noted and the soil pH has been checked in various places. The north point and direction of a prevailing wind are also included.

Below Triangulation really is a very straightforward technique that allows you to easily fix an object that would be difficult to calculate by 'running' measurements. In this case the laburnum tree needs to be accurately plotted and measurements have been taken from either end of the house, the dimensions of which have already been measured. When you prepare the scale drawing you place a compass point on either end of the building and extend a radius, to scale, of the surveyed distance. Where the arcs intersect is the exact position of the laburnum.

TRIANGULATION

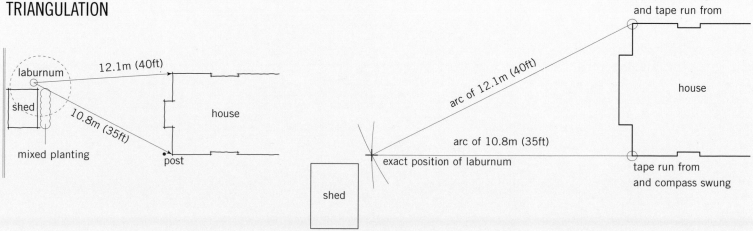

laburnum

12.1m (40ft)

shed

house

10.8m (35ft)

mixed planting

post

compass swung and tape run from

arc of 12.1m (40ft)

house

arc of 10.8m (35ft)

exact position of laburnum

tape run from and compass swung

shed

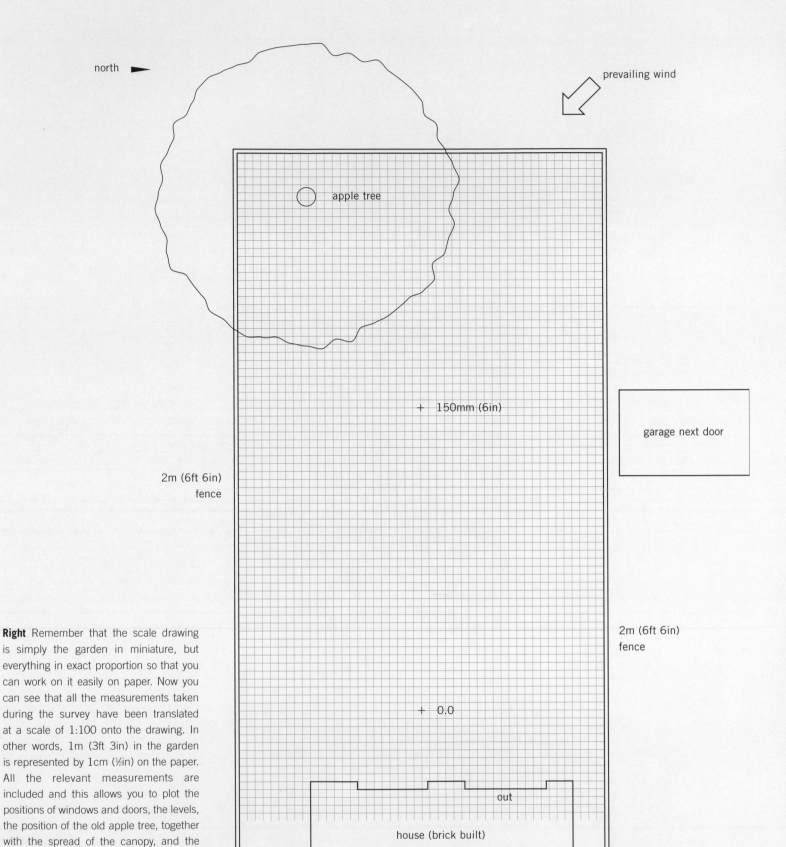

north ►

prevailing wind

apple tree

+ 150mm (6in)

garage next door

2m (6ft 6in)
fence

2m (6ft 6in)
fence

+ 0.0

out

house (brick built)

Right Remember that the scale drawing is simply the garden in miniature, but everything in exact proportion so that you can work on it easily on paper. Now you can see that all the measurements taken during the survey have been translated at a scale of 1:100 onto the drawing. In other words, 1m (3ft 3in) in the garden is represented by 1cm (½in) on the paper. All the relevant measurements are included and this allows you to plot the positions of windows and doors, the levels, the position of the old apple tree, together with the spread of the canopy, and the garage next door. The north point is clearly shown and also the direction of the prevailing wind.

Making a scale drawing

Many people have difficulty in understanding scales or a scale drawing. Essentially it involves creating a picture of your garden in miniature. Everything in that picture will be in proportion so that each feature or surface can be worked out accurately.

An easy way to visualize things would be to have a scale of 1:1, which is exactly the same size as the garden, rather impractical in terms of a drawing on the kitchen table. A scale of 1:2 would be half the size of the garden, 1:4 a quarter of the size, and so on. Realistically, for a small garden a scale of 1:50 is normal; in other words the drawing is fifty times smaller than the garden, but in exact proportion to it.

Now we need to transfer the measurements and other information we gathered onto a piece of paper so that we can get down to the exciting job of planning the garden.

Graph paper is the easiest to use as this is divided into neat squares, each or a number of which, can represent a foot or metre on the ground. Before you start, work out whether the garden will fit on the piece of graph paper. At a scale of 1:50, 2cm (¾in) on the scale drawing will represent 1m (3ft 3in) on the ground. So if we have a garden that is 10m (33ft) long and 5m (16ft) wide this would occupy 20cm x 10cm (8in x 4in) on the graph paper.

Now we can start to transfer measurements. Looking at your survey, you can now easily translate the running measurements into a scale of 1:50. If the edge of the house is say 1.5m (5ft) in from the boundary this will be drawn as a measurement of 3cm (1¼in) on your scale drawing. If one side of a window is at 3m (10ft), this will scale off at 6cm (2½in). The other side of the window might be 4m (13ft) from the boundary, so is drawn at 8cm (3in) on the scale drawing (you can see this principle in the running measurements shown on page 25). If the boundaries are not square and run off at an angle, or you need to plot the position of a tree, use the triangulation technique.

Very soon you will see the whole garden take shape: often it looks quite different drawn to scale than how you actually perceive it when standing outside. This will allow you to develop a design that takes account of the actual dimensions rather than what you think they might be. It's amazing how often I prepare a design, take it back to my clients and they can't believe that the garden is actually that shape. Perception and reality are very influential at this conceptual stage.

On the scale drawing you should also mark in all the other information you gathered, the direction of a prevailing wind, changes of level, the materials used for boundaries and their heights, views, existing planting, the north point, and so on. By now I'll bet you know your garden a lot better than most other people know their own. You have gone through the same process as a professional designer, having at your fingertips and on your scale drawing all the information necessary to create a design. Some might say that this is long winded, but it is far from that. By doing a survey you will have gotten right inside the spirit of the place and, believe you me, gardens have spirit and character in abundance. Now you have the exciting job of melding it into something just perfect for you all.

Above Planting can often completely disguise the shape of a garden. See how this uncompromising rectangle has been softened so you hardly know where the boundaries are; a perfect oasis in the city.

Budgets

At this point you need to think about a sensible budget figure. Gardens, like most other things, don't just happen, they need paying for. When moving home the house usually, and quite understandably, takes priority. In turn this often means that available budgets get swallowed up in various changes and improvements. All I would really like to say here is that *if* you can put a sum aside for use later it will be enormously helpful.

Many people underestimate the cost of building a garden and, while this need not be horrendous, you should be realistic. Naturally a small garden is limited in space but, on the other hand, it will probably rely more heavily on the hard landscape elements of paving, walling and other built-in space-saving features. These invariably take the lion's share of any budget and could be up to 75 per cent of the total figure. Hard landscape works are akin to building costs on the house itself, and most of us are aware of what these can add up to. Plants and planting are relatively inexpensive, but still cost money – just because weeds grow free does not mean that everything else does.

One advantage that your garden may have is that you can construct it in several stages, using the design as a template so that you do not lose track of the original idea. If you like, this could be a bolt-on concept, with different stages being tackled over a period of time, but with each leading on from and adding to the last. I often suggest this approach to clients and it works well, allowing the cost to be spread over a sensible period. It is an old adage that no one wants a garden design but everyone wants a finished garden, but you can see how important the former would be in such a situation.

At the end of the day it all comes down to priorities; how important is your garden or yard to you? I'd argue that it is equally as important as your lounge or dining room or perhaps even kitchen. It will, in reality, probably be all of these, as well as play space, growing area, utility room or even bedroom. All this for the price of, say, a new kitchen!

Refining your wish list

Your list might include an ample sitting area, raised beds, water in one of a million guises, overheads smothered with fragrant climbers, shed, compost bin, lawn – yes, even a tiny garden can have one if planned properly. You might want planting to soften the boundaries and drift the view on to a more distant place or landscape; dividers to create a feeling of greater space; play equipment or a sandpit while the children are growing up; one or more trees to cast dappled shade or screen a bad view; room for herbs or vegetables. The list goes on and it does not matter in the slightest if it gets too long at this stage; we can always thin it down later, homing in on the most important priorities.

Now is also the time to think about some of the other essentials, for example, lighting that will transform the space at night and extend the time that we can enjoy it. No need to work out a scheme yet, or look at different lighting techniques – you can only do that once the design is complete – but you can certainly budget for it. Irrigation too can be a huge help in getting young plants established, or keeping things going if you live in a hot climate or situation. Small gardens are often surrounded by high boundaries and overhung with roofs, making it hard for rain to reach all the planted areas. A well-conceived irrigation scheme might make all the difference. Even in cool temperate countries a roof garden or balcony has a harsh climate that will benefit from extra help.

By now you will have a wealth of information at your fingertips. You have watched and waited with the turning of the seasons, you have made a survey, identified existing plant material, started to see the good and not so good points of the garden and, most importantly, started to think about the *kind* of composition you want.

The time has come, at last, to roll all this together into a design and that is just what we are going to look at next, dispelling a few myths along the way.

Below People are often afraid of using rectangles in a garden, thinking them to be hard and unsympathetic. They can be beautifully elegant, one shape interlocking with another to build up a fascinating pattern that can be softened by planting.

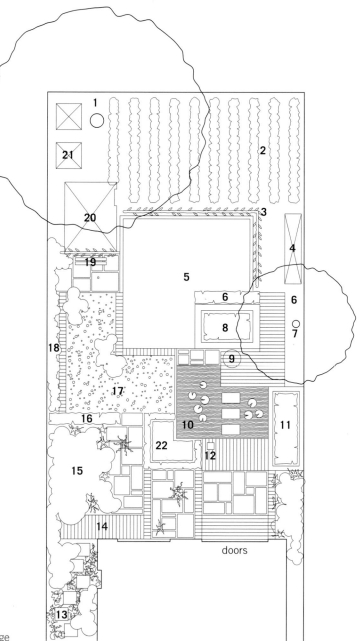

KEY

1 Old apple tree
2 Vegetables
3 Espalier fruit
4 Cold frame
5 Lawn
6 Yew hedge 1.8m (6ft) high
7 *Rhus typhina laciniata*
8 Raised bed 450mm (18in) high
9 Pot
10 Pool
11 Raised bed 450mm (18in) high

12 Statue
13 Path to front garden
14 Brick paving
15 Mixed planting
16 Yew hedge 1.8m (6ft) high
17 Gravel
18 Climbers on fence
19 Seat backed by trellis
20 Shed
21 Compost
22 Herbs surrounded by low box hedge

Architecture in the garden

Much garden design relies on a strong sense of geometry, something that is immediately apparent in this small urban yard, designed by Stephen Woodhams, a talented contemporary garden designer. As in the best compositions, there is a wonderful linkage and flow of space from inside to outside. This is initially set up by the clean lines of the conservatory that allow light and views to flood into this first outside room. Humour is an indispensable element of much good design and here an artificial green lawn offers a subtle horticultural hint that helps to draw you into the garden. Stepping stones cross the shallow pool, setting up reflections from both inside and out in the floor-to-ceiling sliding glass doors. Across the water there is ample room for sitting, dining and entertaining, and here the geometry of the design comes into its own. Decking is laid so the joints lead the eye into the garden, reinforced by the clean lines of the no-nonsense pre-cast concrete paving. Both decking and paving overhang the water slightly, creating interesting shadows. The deck is precisely aligned with the low raised bed, vertical boards exactly matching their flooring counterparts, while the pattern is repeated with the vertical slats on the far boundary.

Repetition is an important part of this garden and a particularly successful feature is the line of circular raised beds, constructed from low-cost concrete sewage rings that normally lie buried

Above Sempervivums have an inherently neat character, making them the perfect choice in this little raised bed set within the architectural theme of the wider garden. They ask for little in the way of maintenance and are resistant to the atmospheric pollution of the city.

Right There is something about crossing water that always brings a slight hesitation, harking back to moated castles! Here it is a perfect device for generating reflections and also allows the stepping stones to give the appearance of gently floating across the surface of the water.

Opposite Imaginative use of materials linked to positive colour theming brings the garden alive in a practical way. While the overall space is limited, it has been organized to allow room for outdoor living.

Above Cannas are wonderful plants and are useful in so many situations. Here they offer architectural form and amazing colour that is repeated elsewhere in the house and garden.

Right Conservatories make the perfect link between inside and out, providing somewhere to bask on a sunny winter's day or an invitation to step into a cool garden in the height of summer.

Opposite There is a wonderful symmetry in these powerful concrete containers, enhanced by the subtle uplighting that warms the unyielding surface.

beneath the streets. Here they are brought into full view, with the maker's name becoming part of the design statement, the lettering aligned to reinforce the repetitive pattern. Such containers are wonderful for planting as they are inexpensive and generously proportioned, allowing a cool deep root run for virtually any form of planting. Annuals cascade over the rims while climbers scramble up surrounding walls, providing a green and fragrant mantle.

Containers figure high in the overall composition, the tall, tapering pots boosting clipped box balls to eye level around the perimeter. Colour adds yet another dimension and this has been as cleverly themed. Warmth is encouraged by the use of a soft orange that is initiated inside the conservatory and then picked up outside with the table and amply sized parasol. The architectural canna lilies continue the hue while the concrete rings are cleverly bottom lit with a warm orange glow that suffuses the textured surface.

All in all, this is a highly organized garden that couples a sophisticated use of space with low maintenance and easy living. It suits both its inner city setting and the needs of a busy owner. It is perhaps the perfect example of practising what you preach.

KEY
1 Stacked sewage rings
2 Timber decking
3 Cobbles
4 Pool
5 Stepping stones
6 Tall pots and box balls
7 Pre-cast concrete paving slabs
8 Tree and planting
9 Timber screen
10 Hedge 1m (3ft 3in) high

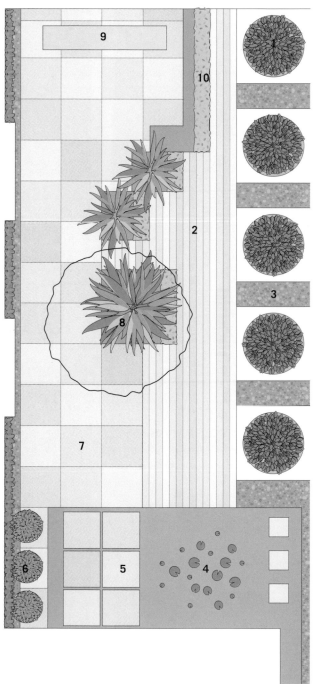

Above From this angle it is easy to see the well-organized changes in level that divide the garden into quite different areas, each with its own character and ambience. Steps are cleanly and simply formed, while the contrast between the low-growing iris and the tall bamboos offers subtle counterpoint.

Right Glass is at last coming into its own in terms of exterior design, providing reflections that are akin to water but in situations and levels where the latter would be impossible. The interplay between the polished surfaces and the granular nature of the crushed marble helps bring this space alive.

Garden of reflections

This is a very cool garden that displays the touch and style of a master craftsman. I use this description quite intentionally as traditionally such people were a combination of builder and architect, having an innate understanding of the design they were creating and the materials at their disposal. That this garden is very much of the twenty-first century matters little, for good and great design is timeless, as the Japanese have shown us for many centuries. The inspiration for this composition is born very much from the philosophy of the latter and anyone interested in the development of contemporary garden design as an art form could do no better than study the work being undertaken by gifted designers of that country.

The essence of the Japanese garden is the paring away of excess and ornamentation, bringing the composition to a point of sublime purity. Religious symbolism is a part of this process, but it is arguable that purity of thought and creation in any work of art amounts to much the same thing.

This garden is an enclosed court and the number of elements chosen for the design are few, comprising concrete, glass, fibre optic lighting, crushed green marble chippings and brass. Access is from two directions, on one side from the glass door set within the clean lines of the metal framed

Above Looking down onto the waterslide and the steps, this is abstract art very much in the footsteps of Mondrian, except that the waterslide is set at a slight angle to the underlying floor and building grid. It is this that brings subtlety and movement to the composition, providing the unexpected rather than the obvious.

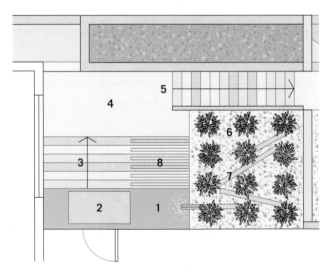

Above Here the four main elements of the garden – bonded glass, crushed stone, water and soaring bamboos – are brought together. It is interesting that the elements of movement, the bamboo and water, are offset by the static materials of glass and stone. This achieves balance, another vital dynamic in exterior design.

Above right So many gardeners are afraid of minimalism, fearing it can eliminate the use of plants. The point, of course, is that it reduces the use of all materials and allows the purity of the design to shine through. In this situation there is a logical extension of the architectural forms into the garden pattern.

KEY

1 Pool
2 Stepping stone
3 Steps
4 Landing
5 Steps
6 Bamboos planted through crushed green marble
7 Glass 'planks'
8 Planting of iris

wall and from the other by a simple flight of concrete steps, cantilevered from the adjoining wall. It is this inherent movement through the space that adds to the overall interest as the views and perception change from one level to another.

It would be easy to label this garden with a design style of, say, minimalist, but my interpretation is that the designer has felt his way through the design process to create a series of levels, angles, spaces and reflective surfaces that complement one another perfectly. This is a highly sophisticated piece of work and in the delicate spatial control, little has been left to chance.

The interplay between the hard landscape materials is both dramatic and subtle, and it is the contrast between the long, rectangular bonded glass planks and the green chippings that immediately draws the eye, leading it across the court to the waterslide and pool that flank the doorway. Such a linear pattern emphasizes the horizontal plane and this is offset by the stems of bamboo that are placed in a controlled grid that reaches up towards the light.

To many gardeners, the use of just two plant species – bamboo and iris – would be an anathema but again it is this simplicity of choice and simple contrast of forms that work so well within the overall framework. Here is proof of the old adage 'less is more' and a greater proportion of planting in this instance would have simply clouded the picture. It is worth remembering that a garden is primarily a space and although many of us expect to see plants in such a situation, they are not always necessary.

This is not a place for rowdy entertainment, rather the quiet contemplation of a fine work of art. Such gardens are few and they should be enjoyed for what they are.

Above At night the garden is transformed into strongly contrasting ground forms with the delicacy of the bamboo stems feathering into a black sky. Fibre optics trace glow-worms of light through the glass planks, heightening the feeling of perspective. Shadows add to the drama, each stone and stem standing out in a sharp relief that is not possible in the softer light of day.

2

PLANNING YOUR GARDEN

Styles and influences

We live in an increasingly mass-produced world – everything from fast food, clothes, cars and even homes. It is all the more refreshing then, that the garden is our own place, a space that we can design ourselves as an entirely unique composition.

Personality

You could have an infinite number of plots, identical in every way, but all would be different simply because of the personality of their owners. Here is a wonderful opportunity to have exactly what you want and not just an approximation you can reach down off the shelf. This is where style, taste, eclecticism, fun and perhaps a little eccentricity can come into play. Of course, there will be inspiration from any number of sources, as well as demands and possible limitations imposed by your family and the site itself. But at the end of it all it will be yours and yours alone: something that is both exciting and possibly slightly daunting in this pre-packaged age.

Style

The starting point for any design is the question of style. This will almost certainly be a combination of your own personal tastes and the underlying architecture of your home. It is unlikely that a crisp period house with a balanced façade will look comfortable fronting a leading-edge deconstructivist garden, or thinking that a striking steel and glass building will be in harmony with the winding paths and lush planting of a country garden. There is nothing wrong with either of these themes, just that they will be out of place in the context I have described.

    As I said earlier, it is likely you chose your house because of its character and location. And you will almost certainly have furnished and decorated it to enhance its style in a way personal to yourself. There is a difference, however, between style and influence, and this is something that a lot of people get mixed up. In my thinking at least, influence is to do with regional or geographical factors. For example, you might have an Italianate, Japanese or cottage garden. These particular influences could also be formal, asymmetric or freeform. In other words, influence is modified or governed by style. This actually makes things simpler and means that there

Above Formality relies on balance and regularity within the design which can bring great strength to the composition. Here the clipped hedges, bold path and traditional seat create a strong perspective.

Right Overlapping sections of deck climb the slope of this yard, subtly offset and balanced by bold planting. This carefully worked asymmetric design offers all the elements of the ideal outside room.

are only four main design styles to consider: formal, asymmetric, freeform – and right out at the artistic limits – deconstructivist.

Before we get too involved, I'm the first to admit that there are many exceptionally talented amateur designers or gardeners who have created the most stunning compositions without any preconceived notion of a particular style. That their work falls into one of these categories is largely immaterial. I do think it is helpful, however, to have an understanding of how the various styles work and how they can be related to your house and what you want from your garden.

Below Although there is a real feeling of eclecticism here, a common bond provided by the tumble of stone, running water and lush planting ties the design together in a thoroughly positive way.

Formal gardens

Formality is perhaps the easiest garden style to understand as it simply relies on balance and repetition from one side or end to the other – imagine two identical pages of a book with a fold between them so that one mirrors the other precisely. Formal gardens tend to be relatively rigid affairs which can be either enhanced or softened by your choice of planting. The best can be gloriously architectural, subtly divided and full of interest; the worst are simply bland.

The layout of such a garden, particularly when contained within a small space, may be elegant but it does impose limitations. This would be a place to

Below Although the ground plan may be regular in a formal design, planting need not follow suit. Here the contrast between beds and hard landscaping reinforce rather than detract from the pool and rills.

sit, dine, contemplate and stroll, rather than being designed for activity, children or boisterous games. Such designs naturally lend themselves to classical architecture, where the doors and windows of the house or apartment leading into the garden are regularly spaced and of similar proportions. Ornaments such as urns or statues are usually used either singly, at the end of a walk or view, or in pairs to flank a doorway or steps or placed either side of a specific feature such as a seat or arbour. The whole essence is one of regularity, control and a measured pace of life.

There was a time when I avoided designing such gardens like the plague, but with age and experience I find I am increasingly drawn to their precision. Formal designs need not necessarily be period pieces; there has been great interest of late in creating formal gardens in the most modern idiom. These often use water, clipped hedging, reflective surfaces and colour in dynamic ways. There is huge scope for bringing this style thoroughly up to date.

Above Austerity is often in the eye of the beholder and what one person may consider severe, another may simply accept as neat, orderly or simple. In this garden, although both the paving and planting are symmetrical and rigidly controlled in the small, enclosed area, the design is really a study in the sculptural manipulation of space.

Asymmetric gardens

While formal design is steeped in history and can trace its roots back to the Romans, Greeks and beyond, there came a time towards the beginning of the twentieth century when artists, architects and designers generally started to question its validity. They found it too rigid: it stultified original thought. During the 1920s a remarkable design school was formed in Germany known as the Bauhaus, under the leadership of Walter Gropius. It included many of the great architects, painters and designers of the day and their efforts were directed towards a new kind of integrated design, where different disciplines worked together. Hitler closed down the Bauhaus after only a few years, but the seeds of the Modern Movement had been sown and many of the masters and students emigrated to America where the movement flourished. Much of their activity was focused in the Bay Area of San Francisco, with designers such as Thomas Church, Dan Kiley and Garrett Eckbo. Here, with a warm climate, the concept of the outside room was born; gardens became places in which to relax, entertain, play and enjoy yourself. The modern garden relied on asymmetry to realize the potential of this new way of living.

Asymmetry is very much to do with both balance and linking with the adjoining house. There is no diminishing of clear architectural rules or principles and in the best designs house and garden flow seamlessly together. Balance in a formal scheme is rigidly mirrored from one side to the other; asymmetry also uses this principle but with features and objects of different visual weight in different parts of the garden. For example, the shape and size of the house may be offset and projected by a terrace set on a grid determined by the architecture of the building (see page 50). In turn the terrace, and quite possibly also the underlying grid, will relate to the shape of the garden itself and the volume of the paving may be balanced by a bold plant bed, lawn or tree. You can compare this to a modernist painting by Mondrian, where the geometry of the canvas is divided into coloured rectangles that set up an endlessly fascinating pattern.

Asymmetry is just as controlled as formalism, but in a much freer way. Precision is everything and the real joy of the style is this wonderfully sensitive manipulation of space that can be adapted to virtually any situation. For this reason it is still very much a design solution for the twentieth and twenty-first century. Modernism may be 75 years old now, but in the hands of a good designer is as fresh now as it ever was.

Above Mondrian, who was one of the great artists of the Modern Movement, had and continues to exert an enormous influence on three-dimensional design. In this small garden, all the classic Modernist principles are illustrated through the considered use of proportional space, simple blocks of colour and perfect asymmetrical balance; the pool is simply a bonus!

Right Irrespective of whether gardens are ancient or modern, many of the same design principles should be applied. Here contemporary steel beams link the house and garden while the crisp, upright rectangle that frames the boundary is really a contemporary 'moongate' (see page 61) that helps to draw the background planting into the composition.

Freeform gardens

Freeform shapes are just that – their outlines do not rely on geometry. Here are amoebic fluid patterns that swirl and slide over one another. They gain their inspiration from the natural world rather than manipulated or created forms: the shapes of cloud banks, meandering river valleys, lowland landscapes or the intricate and beautiful tracery of leaf forms. Designers are increasingly exploring the possibilities of all these and creating gardens of great worth. The style is far from easy to handle well and needs a sensitive eye for form, shape and balance. The important thing to remember is that the finished picture will have to relate not only to itself but all that is around it, including the boundaries, borrowed landscape and most importantly, the adjoining building.

In a small garden the effect can be breathtaking. It could be built up from lush jungle-like planting that conceals any hint of a boundary, with sinuous pathways snaking through and around the garden. Alternatively, a composition could be unashamedly upbeat, with swirling beds of grasses and hardy perennials set about with pathways of gravel and lawns of glass beads that dance and dazzle in the sun.

Much of the secret of designing in small spaces is to do with containment – both of the place itself and keeping interest within the garden's boundaries. Freeform and deconstructivist design (see pages 48–49) have huge potential to achieve this.

Left If the rigidity of walls is ignored in a tiny garden and the design turned in upon itself to create a fluid a freeform pattern, you can create a wonderful feeling of space that quite literally flows from place to place. That this lushly planted area has been created within the restrains of a roof garden is all the more remarkable as many people would be hard pressed to achieve such a delightful effect at ground level.

Right Of all garden elements, water has a wonderful ability to soften all around it. Movement, reflections, aquatic planting and, of course, wildlife can bring such a feature alive, providing either a focal point or, as here, a pivot for the whole garden.

Deconstructivist gardens

Deconstructivism is at the outer limits of garden design. This is pure art that takes all the rules, disassembles them and then rearranges them into patterns that may be subtle, stimulating or downright aggressive! Like any artist, you have to know what you are doing in all of this: you can't break the rules without knowing what they are in the first place. Deconstructivist gardens at horticultural shows bring sobs of disbelief from the conventional and whoops of joy from those who are looking for something fresh or different. Like good sculpture, such compositions elicit strong reactions, and as an art form they are entirely valid.

Geometry will almost certainly be the driving force, but using angles, proportions and lines that set out to challenge the conventional. Materials will almost certainly be leading edge with steel, plastic and glass figuring high on the agenda. Water can be used in endlessly fascinating ways and sculpture naturally will have a real role to play. Plants, yes plants, will bring counterpoint and although many died-in-the-wool horticulturists cringe at such gardens, they can be a wonderful synthesis of planting, geometric forms and well-planned outside living space.

By looking at the possibilities of different styles you can start to see that there is a good deal of potential both in your garden and in the way you approach a design solution. I also think that by now you can appreciate that the style you choose will be a subtle combination of the personality of you and your family, your house, your interior design preferences and your lifestyle generally.

Left If you wish to experiment with shapes, form and spatial relationships, you have to know what you are doing. There is a real dialogue here that allows the path, stonework, variable height screen and planting to work as one, something that underlines the Zen influence.

Right Optical illusions have been used in the modelling of both interior and exterior space since the dawn of design. Initially you think that these forms are positioned within a horizontal surface when in fact the whole feature is a mirror waterfall set about with cubes and rectangles hung off the face of a wall.

Right The levels were initially very awkward in this small garden, climbing both up and then to the right. The owners wanted minimal maintenance but with a crisp, contemporary design. Moving away from the house there is an ample paved area for sitting and barbecuing, the paving helping to lead the eye out into the garden and towards the first broad step. At this point I turned the design at a diagonal to the boundaries so you climb in two directions, taking your time to reach the deck that is situated at the highest level to take advantage of the evening sun. Overhead beams are hung from a high boundary wall and these, together with climbers, break the outline of the former. Planting softens and surrounds the retaining walls, steps and garden generally, providing colour and interest throughout the year.

KEY
1 *Betula jacquemontii*
2 Overhead beams and climbers
3 Seat
4 Climbers on high wall
5 Stepping stones
6 Mixed planting
7 Brick edge to steps
8 Pre-cast concrete paving
9 Retaining wall
10 *Robinia pseudoacacia* 'Frisia'
11 Brick paving
12 Mixed planting
13 Mixed planting

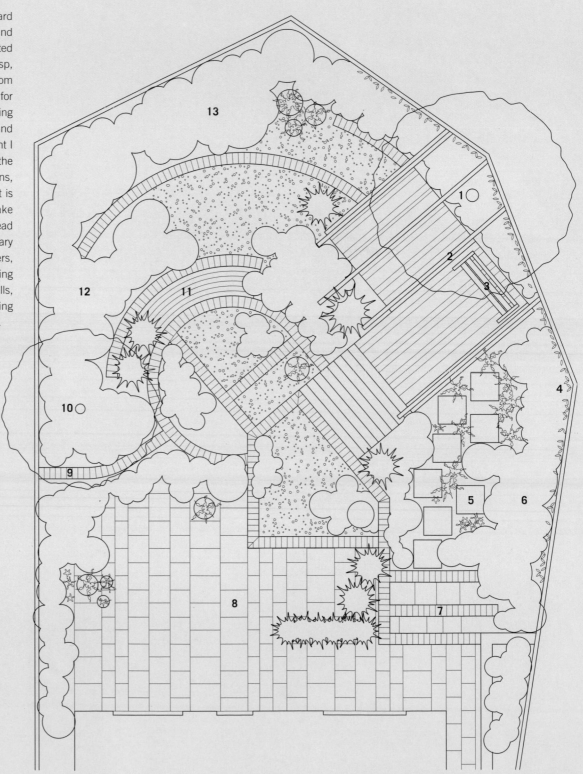

Making your ideas come to life

Having considered the style of garden, we have now reached the stage in the design process where it is time to start putting all this theory into practice. This is the real business, the fun and exciting part. We can go about this in a number of different ways, partly drawing the design out on paper and partly pegging out shapes and temporarily erecting screens and dividers outside, so that we can really start to visualize how the surfaces, spaces and shapes will eventually relate to one another. I have made the point already, fairly forcefully, that exterior design is much to do with pattern making. In turn, that pattern will naturally be based on the style that you choose for the garden, the framework provided by the house or apartment on one side and the surrounding boundaries on the others. As we usually enter the garden from the house, the boundaries will have much to do with the final garden layout.

Using grids

Many designers, myself included, often take the outline or 'footprint' of the building and project lines from it out into the surrounding space. With a regular façade, this could form a regularly spaced projection of lines. By taking this same dimension and turning it at right angles, we form a grid of similarly sized squares. This then can form the basis for a ground plan of different surfaces, just like a Mondrian painting. Not all the grid squares need contain different materials; if they did, this would make for an uncomfortably busy pattern. Instead a number can be grouped together to form a paved area, a lawn or raised beds.

Alternatively, if a house does not have a regular outline but has projecting bays, for example, these can still form the basis of a grid. In this case, however, it will set up altogether different dynamics, which can be very interesting to work with. Let me add a word of caution here – don't allow yourself to become too fixated on grid systems. If a grid makes sense by helping to project the building into the garden, then that's all well and good, but sometimes this does not work at all and you need to look for another solution.

A variation on the grid method might be to turn the whole pattern at an angle to the house. Very often you will have a bay window, or in modern architecture a prow, that juts out into the garden. So often this is ignored in landscape terms, which can be a missed opportunity. Seize it, project your design lines out from it and match the resulting angles. You will discover a whole new set of dynamics opening up and creating a diagonal pattern that is full of potential (see the diagram on the facing page for how this can be worked to your advantage). It is a well-known design fact that a diagonal line is the longest distance across a rectangle. Using such a pattern in a garden of the same shape tends to increase the overall feeling of space, a useful trick of the trade and invaluable when planning a small space garden.

Garden shapes

Naturally enough, the shape of the garden has a real influence on the overall design. It is something you cannot change so you have to learn how to work with it and make the most of it.

Long, narrow gardens

Long, narrow spaces are ideal for subdivision and can form a wonderful progression as you move through them. Use divisions to create separate garden rooms, with the opportunity to theme each in a particular way. This might, in a family situation, be driven by practicality. In one of our gardens, when the children were young I planned the first outside room as a paved terrace adjoining the house (see page 104). Here was room for sitting and dining, space for wheeled toys and a portable sandpit that could be moved into the sun or shade. All of this was clearly visible from the kitchen window. From here, broad steps dropped down to one side of the terrace and a path led down the garden flanking a lawn large enough for play. At the bottom of the path I placed a seat, as a focal point, somewhere to watch the children or simply to relax. The seat acted both as punctuation in the design and turned the path at right angles across the space, where it dropped again into an area of old fruit trees, rougher grass and naturalized bulbs. Right at the bottom of the garden, screened by the trees, was the utility area including shed, compost heap, incinerator and all those other necessary things. So, in a long, narrow and relatively confined space I had created four quite separate areas and the garden felt far larger as a result. We moved before the children grew up but this arrangement could easily have been modified in later years to accept more delicate and differently themed planting and I had intended to convert one of the larger raised beds into a pond. However, this shows that a garden can be dramatically changed in character or overall look without making expensive alterations to the basic layout.

In the garden described above, I used a basic rectangular design for each of the areas, albeit much softened by plentiful planting. Curving shapes based on radii would have been just as appropriate, with the path sweeping from side to side to create a real feeling of space and movement.

While this kind of long narrow garden is easy to deal with, many people get into real difficulties when the shape is turned the other way so that the narrowest part is directly opposite the house.

Above Linearity is a powerful visual magnet in many gardens, emphasized here by the simple planting and red tiled path that draws the eye quickly down to the blue gate at the far end. This has been created as a measured statement and underlines the importance of colour – if the gate was brown it would have blended into the background and lost the effect altogether.

Wide, short gardens

Such plots inevitably feel smaller than they really are, so plan them carefully. The worst thing that you can do here is to place some kind of focal point in full view of the windows looking out onto the garden. This simply has the effect of drawing the eye and foreshortening the space still further. The secret of success is to soften the immediate boundary with planting, perhaps using the borrowed landscape trick of blending it into a garden beyond (see page 14). Then place your major point of interest towards one end of the garden. In this way you may catch a glimpse of it from inside the house and when you move outside, you are drawn to it down the longest dimension of the plot. Visual space is maximized to full effect, the views are opened up and the short boundary instantly becomes far less dominant.

Square gardens

In a square garden, things are altogether more static. There are two solutions here, the first of which is to capitalize on its shape and build on a basic rectangle with further overlapping rectangles. This is like a simple student abstract art project and you can try it yourself by placing sheets of paper over one another to build up endlessly different permutations. Alternatively, take

Above This garden is wider than it is deep, a problem that can be particularly difficult to solve. The secret is not to place a focal point opposite the house but to lead the eye to one side or the other, thus bringing the longest dimension into play. Here the gravel is contained within oval brickwork that leads the eye quite naturally to the seat, framed by planting.

a piece of graph paper, which is already neatly divided into squares, and draw a series of overlapping rectangles. Then do just the same thing with your scale drawing of your garden (see page 29).

The other, quite opposite way to handle a square is to disguise the boxy shape and right angles completely by creating a fluid shape within the boundaries. At its simplest, this could take the form of a central, circular lawn completely surrounded by abundant planting that in turn hides the boundary walls or fences.

Dog-legged gardens

Most gardens are either rectangular or square but occasionally you come across different shapes. Dog-legged gardens are, in effect, two rectangles butted together, with one disappearing from view where it overlaps a neighbouring garden at right angles or other area to the left or right. This area can be small but this need not detract from its inherent potential. There is the opportunity here to create a feeling of mystery, as the furthest part of the garden will be completely hidden. A path could sweep enticingly away from the house and into a secret garden, where it might lead to a seat, dining area or other feature.

While the garden rooms will indeed be separate and could well have a different purpose or theme, the secret of success will be in how you link them. You want to be beguiled from place to place rather than simply happening on it. It is tempting to use hidden places as a dumping ground or utility area but this is missing out on a real opportunity. Practical elements can always be thoughtfully planned, but a hidden place is a bonus to be worked on and made the very best of.

Triangular gardens

These are relatively common, particularly in an urban situation where gardens are often made up from all kinds of left-over spaces. As with square gardens, there are two ways to handle them.

The strength of a triangle is the apex and if this is directly in front of the viewpoint, then the eye tends to be firmly locked into it. In many ways it is sensible to go with the flow and emphasize this by positioning a major feature right in its corner. The narrowing boundaries will add to the feeling of perspective and make the focal point exceptionally strong. As a direct result of this, the space will feel foreshortened so it is imperative that any feature is well thought out and impeccably

constructed. It could be a water feature, an arbour with seating below, a decorative urn or a fine piece of sculpture. In terms of planting, a single specimen tree or shrub will do much the same thing, riveting the eye and demanding attention. A species with an architectural shape will be the most effective.

This approach is a variation of the formal style and could be reinforced by regularly patterned beds to either side of the garden as it narrows.

A different solution would be to detract from the apex by sweeping the line of a lawn or paved area past in a strong flowing curve. Rather than placing a feature in the corner, use a drift of planting that starts on one side and leads the eye past the apex and back towards the house or viewpoint. If you can conceal the boundary altogether then the dominance of the triangle is lost. By using this approach you are creating one shape within another and manipulating the space accordingly.

Above To divide a small garden can actually increase a feeling of space and the pool helps check the view and slow you down before crossing the stone bridge. To the left, the gateway through the wall creates a real tension point, again slowing you before discovering the next garden room.

Right A slight change of level can add enormous interest to a design and the raised terrace at the end of the garden, paved in Portland stone offers a perfect sitting area. A mirror water feature provides a focal point, standing out in sharp relief against the brick wall.

Left The secret to clever design often lies in the unusual, and this divider has a strong watery feel. There is a link between the partially submerged granite sett path and the vertical line of the screen, heightened by the reflective quality of the water.

Using dividers

The key to nearly all design, in whatever field, is the division and control of space. Within this book you will notice that the page layouts are constructed in a particular way, partly with text and partly with photographs or diagrams. This achieves balance and, as your eye moves from area to area, each block has its own purpose and interpretation. However, a book is only two-dimensional; in a house we naturally move from room to room, each having a separate function. The third dimension comes into play, the walls preventing you from seeing from one place into another. This in turn helps to increase the feeling of space as you stay in any one room for a given time. If you look at a plan of a house, or even better the concrete foundation slab on which it is built before the walls go up, you will be amazed at just how small the overall area is.

One side effect of internal walls is to maximize visual perception. Even in a studio or warehouse conversion with a wide, open-plan layout, the use of moveable screens, colour and carpets helps provide a degree of intimacy that many of us feel necessary. Purists and minimalists may favour a completely unhindered space. There is nothing wrong with this approach either, it is simply different – which is exactly what creativity is all about. On the whole, however, the creation of individual spaces within a larger area will bring a number of key garden design elements into play.

Left Many of the most subtle small gardens are contained and controlled by walls. In this perfect outside room, the pale colour wash on the walls brings a feeling of warmth that is heightened by the Mediterranean planting.

Right Hedges offer a soft and flexible method of controlling space. Here they are clipped in a crisp, formal shape reinforcing the rectangular lawn. The narrow gap between them increases tension, drawing you forward into the next garden room.

Above A glimpse of what lies beyond is often far more effective than a full-on view. There is an interesting link in vertical pattern between the bold Phormium in the foreground and the more delicate *Miscanthus* behind the Perspex screens.

Right A study in the mysterious is heightened by the opaque wall and door that hints at another garden beyond. The positive detailing of the metal framework is impeccable here, perfectly complemented by the planting, in delicate counterpoint.

Tension, mystery and surprise

If we look at our garden room as an empty space it will appear to be just that, lacking a good deal of inherent interest. As soon as we start to introduce dividers, we not only form additional spaces but also control the way in which we get from one place to another.

In the smallest yard just a single wing of wall or trellis, set to one side, makes us move around it. It screens the space beyond and once negotiated, gives the opportunity to discover a different area, feature or focal point. In basic design terms, there is a feeling of mystery as you look towards the screen, a degree of tension as you approach it and then surprise as the barrier is passed and a new view opens up. If wings encroach from either side to form a narrow space then the feelings of tension, mystery and surprise are heightened. Where the wings are exactly in line with one another and perhaps scalloped down to the middle a formal effect is created. Offset screens, with one slightly further away and the other closer to the house, give a feeling of zigzagging down the garden. This pattern can be reinforced by a path that leads down

the garden on one side, turns across the space at a right angle, passing behind a screen, and then turns again at a right angle, for a wonderful sub-division with the path completely disappearing from view.

The permutations of division are endless, as are the materials in which they are made. Brick or stone walls, wooden fences and trellis, hedges, loose planting – all can be effective, but the important thing is the choice in relation to what is around them and the overall garden plan. The cue for a screen can come from the boundary construction, budget permitting. You can, of course, mix and match, and a well-detailed trellis works out a good deal cheaper than a wall. Think of factors like height, too – it will look most uncomfortable if the divider is higher than the boundary.

Colour is important. To my mind, there is far too much nonsense on television makeover programmes with screens or trellis painted quite unsympathetic hues. A blue trellis may be fashionable but it will quickly pall and most likely fade too. Think of the purpose of the feature, which is primarily designed to divide space, not shout at you. In addition, a strongly coloured screen is not the best foil for planting – in fact it will be downright difficult.

Above A wall naturally provides division but the curved shape shown here adds rhythm while the tiled mosaic decoration provides a Gaudiesque touch. Such patination offers colour in a shady place where planting might be difficult, and it emphasizes the importance of considering the different possibilities of decorating vertical surfaces.

The siting of dividers should not be a random process and here your scale drawing will be invaluable. The smallest garden may need only one, placed perhaps to one side. The exact position can be juggled on your plan and then pegged out in the garden for final analysis. I often find it useful to have a few spare trellis panels that can be simply stood in position to see the potential effect. You can easily reposition these before deciding on their final placement.

In architectural terms there is a magic measurement called a golden section. It was formulated by the ancient Greeks and indicates the ideal point at which to divide a line – visually between a third and three-quarters of its length. In a garden this makes for a remarkably comfortable control of space, with something like two thirds of the plot closer to the house and one third at the far end. This could be the perfect place to site your divider or position a seat or focal point. It will be a place to pause, to change direction and essentially a point that adds inherent interest to the overall design.

Above A succession of elegant arches constructed to the same design creates a repetitive pattern that both provides a restful vista and carries your eye quite naturally to the far end of the walkway. The delicate ogee shape offers lightness, drawing the eye upwards towards the sunlight – another useful design trick in a shady place.

In a curvaceous or freeform garden (see pages 46 – 47) the dividers themselves may be curved. This is easily achieved with a newly planted hedge or specially constructed wall but less so with a rigid panel of wooden trellis, so choose the material with the intended shape in mind. Curves could be set in opposition to one another or perhaps in a serpentine pattern, and the shapes could additionally enclose a feature such as statuary or a pool – the permutations here are endless.

If we use the principles of tension, mystery and surprise (see pages 58 – 59), we can reinforce their power through the inclusion of gates, arches and pergolas, all of which have the ability to control space within the outer boundaries.

An archway between two garden rooms that are separated by two wings of a divider serves to reinforce a delicious feeling of tension, the space being positively compressed as you walk below. A gate between garden rooms makes you pause while opening it – another device in the progression of space. A moongate is one of the most tempting visual devices; a circular opening in a wall that allows you to see through but not actually step into the area beyond. Glimpses are always tantalizing and demand to be explored.

Above Although moongates have a long pedigree, they can be just as valuable in garden design today as they ever were. The rounded shape, as shown here, is rather easier on the eye than a rectangular or square opening and, like a ship's porthole, provides a real focus to the view beyond, drawing you towards the next garden room.

Left A disappearing view always asks to be explored and can be a valuable tool in creating movement around the garden. Steps will heighten a feeling of tension and expectation as you move towards them, a new view revealing itself as you reach the top of the flight.

Pergolas

Pergolas make fantastic dividers and are valid even in a small garden. Their charm lies in a journey from one place to another with partial glimpses to either side. They are the perfect vehicle for climbing plants and fragrant species will heighten the experience. Because the plants are the stars, construction should be strong, simple and straightforward. There's no need for frippery and additions such as hanging baskets should be avoided like the plague.

The really important thing about a pergola is that it should not only go somewhere positive but also have a focal point sited at the end. This could be a seat, an urn or statue, or even a water feature: it is depressing when a pergola terminates at a compost heap or the garden shed.

Dividers are one of the major factors in the creation of a garden but don't – and this is desperately important – use them simply for the sake of doing so. Every design should have a purpose: the old battle cry of the Modern Movement of form following function is as pertinent today as it was 75 years ago. There is nothing worse than design for design's sake, but we seem to be plagued by the notion, particularly in the garden.

Above Complete double hoops, softened with abundant planting, make a pergola with a difference and set up a real rhythm as you move beneath them. Such shapes would blend well with a garden built up from circles or curves, cleverly extending the horizontal theme into the vertical.

Right Tunnels, pergolas and arches all belong to the same family, encouraging movement from place to place and providing a feeling of enclosure in the process. Metal is becoming increasingly popular as a construction material in the garden and this elegant curved frame would be ideal host for a collection of climbing plants.

Garden rooms

Dividers create areas and rooms, each of which should embrace a purpose: sitting and dining; play; growing fruit or flowers; utility and so on. The creation of space division is multi-functional, both aesthetic and practical. A simple wing of trellis that divides the garden could also screen a shed, work area or next-door's garage. Take this a stage further and you could build a completely integrated store for tools, bikes, toys and most things. Neatly concealed, reached by passing beneath overheads or an archway smothered with planting, and sensibly blended into the wider garden picture.

The smaller a garden, the harder a feature has to work, so embrace every opportunity to do just that. The important thing is the subtle and sensitive manipulation of space: get it right and your garden will be an infinitely better place as a result. For instance, dividers can be soft as well as hard so a neatly clipped hedge or planting of feathery grasses could be remarkably effective. Think laterally and you might use a narrow pool with water jets or a water curtain falling from above, while at night uplighters can provide subtle and very different space division.

Above The concept of the garden as a room may be something of a cliché but in the right setting is absolutely right. In this small area there is ample space for sitting, dining and generally relaxing.

Left The real difference between rooms inside and outside lies in the degree of planting that brings the latter alive. Strong architectural features such as columns and walls can be softened and blended into a practical yet vibrant space.

Opposite Even the smallest room outside can have many more features and uses than its interior counterpart. How many rooms inside the house could have a stove, water feature, planting on different levels and ample room for sitting?

Changes in levels

When surveying your garden you will have noticed any changes of level and they may well have already had a bearing on your design. The smaller a garden, the more critical any level change will be. A plot that slopes up from the house tends to foreshorten the view while one that slopes away looks slightly larger than it really is.

Any slope will need negotiating but don't think that you necessarily have to chop your garden into a series of steps or terraces. When dealing with only a gentle slope there is nothing worse than a garden designed as a jumble of awkward platforms. In this situation I often design a terrace area immediately adjoining the house, then step up or down onto the next level which, whether lawn or planting, can be gently graded with the natural fall

Above Steps generally should be as broad, generous and easy-going as possible, which not only offers practicality but makes them a feature in their own right. The steps that link the two levels in this garden are emphasized by the planting that acts as a natural focus. The pleached limes in the background are an attractive idea, softening the façade of the house.

Right Shallow, curvaceous steps set up their own rhythm and offer a less formal link between levels than a straight flight. In order to soften the transition each stone tread has been separated from the next by a gently sloping grass ramp, something the great Canadian architect Arthur Erickson calls 'stramps'.

of the land. If the slope is steeper, make each terrace or flat area as generous as you can, linking each with broad steps. In a garden where the change of level is not great, the whole area can be a series of large steps or platforms, one overlapping the next, interwoven and surrounded with planting.

Steps should never be mean, awkward or dangerous in a garden – they can often run the full width of the plot or area you are dealing with. The permutations for construction are endless, but there is a comfortable size step that feels just right. The tread, the part you walk on, should be 45cm (18in) deep and the riser or upright section, 15cm (6in) high. This is slightly less than a stair in the house. Wide steps can show off pots and ornaments, as well as providing great occasional seats. Where space permits, a flight of steps can change direction part way up the slope. Usually this will be at right angles and a small landing can again offer room for pots and other incidental features.

Space can be severely limited at times, for example, a narrow flight of steps down to a basement area in a tiny town garden. Safety is paramount and if there is not a good handrail then fix one. Pots can be used to soften the steps but if the area is just too narrow try plants growing up a flanking wall from the lowest level or cascading down from the top from a built-in bed.

Eclecticism is a good thing in a garden. While it can flavour the overall composition, it can also be extended to the choice of landscaping materials. I know of one stunning garden that has a Moorish theme where the steps and other features are faced with brightly coloured tiles.

Above The delicacy of these made-to-measure metal steps allows them to 'float' from one level to another, widening as they approach the bottom. Such an open flight allows plants to be grown around and underneath, adding to their ethereal character. Strong handrails add safety while the no-nonsense deck offers a spacious landing.

Retaining walls

Steps provide access but a slope offers all kinds of other possibilities. In many situations a retaining wall may rear up in front of you, which can be overpowering to say the least. But it is a great opportunity to use the structure as a background or support for something else. Built-in seating could easily be tucked into the angle of two walls, as could a barbecue. Both options have storage potential and I often design barbecues with worktops, beneath which are cupboards for tools, gas bottles or anything else. Seats too will have room within and you might have a hinged top that could store toys – great for a quick tidy up when people come round unexpectedly.

On the subject of play and toys, a raised platform is ideal for youngsters; they will use it as a table, jump off it, make an improvized slide and so on. If the area is paved with smooth slabs it will be easy to clean off. I also like raised sandpits, fitted with a removable cover, that might later be converted into a pool or raised bed. Raised beds boost planting to an intermediate level that will then grow up and tumble down to soften the whole structure. My own garden slopes quite steeply. In the first change of level, close to both the house and the street, I have built in a refuse store that backs neatly against a retaining wall. The top of the store is paved in brick and is big enough for a group of pots while timber double doors keep it looking neat. It can be useful to think laterally in such situations. In a garden where space is at a premium, you need to take advantage of every opportunity. If a feature can be multi-purpose, so much the better.

A retaining wall can be a good opportunity to create a water feature, either cascading from one level to another or, if space is limited, as a wall-hung feature spouting into a bowl below. You do not need a huge feature for maximum effect: often the sound of a simple bubble fountain is perfect. Water has the ability to add another dimension to a garden with reflection, movement and sound. Even in a tiny yard it is able to draw the eye, increasing the feeling of space.

Below Although powerfully designed, the raised beds have a real delicacy in the detailing, which fits perfectly with the decking and gravel panels and creates a subtle colour harmony between the *Stachys* and the walls.

Water features

Water is a natural element in many gardens and offers the scope to provide a real focal point. Time was when such features were confined to quasi-classical cherubs spouting – or worse – into bowls. While such a feature may still be valid in a formal design, there is now a huge choice of more contemporary ideas. Some of the most beautiful use reflective surfaces such as stainless steel, where water is pumped up and slides down the surface in ever-changing patterns. They may be wave shapes, columns or bowls with water spilling into a pool below.

Glass, too, is becoming more widely used and mirrors or mirrored acrylic can look stunning with water sliding down the face. Reflective surfaces are useful in a small yard as they produce images that create a feeling of greater space. The fact that these images are distorted is even better, as they blur reality and don't look too obvious.

Above Many of the most successful water features are refreshingly simple and this raised bubble acts as both a focal point in this tiny yard as well as raised area perfect for sitting. There is an interesting dialogue between the no-nonsense design and the feathery bamboos, the cushions adding their own splash of colour. Maintenance is kept to a minimum with easy care paving and a much of small cobbles over the planted areas.

Left This is the classic example of how two quite different concepts can be brought into harmony. While the background planting is lushly soft the metal edged water feature is strikingly architectural, the foreground boulder adding a powerful counterpoint.

Special effects

Above Mirrors used in a city roof garden can be absolutely stunning, reflecting an intriguing and eclectic jumble of townscape that adds both depth and a double take to any composition. The only thing you have to be extremely careful about is solar reflection as there is nothing worse than walking into a blinding light from a shaded interior.

Built-in features can save space in practical terms, but there is absolutely nothing wrong in creating an illusion of space too. Such effects have a long and distinguished pedigree, being much used in gardens and architecture since the earliest times. The real point in all these features – trompe l'oeil, mirrors, false perspectives, murals and much more – is that they are a visual trick, and not to be taken seriously. I personally cannot abide chic town gardens where false perspective trellis is stuck on the wall with a pretentious cherub or insipid Aphrodite as a focal point. This smacks of horticultural snobbery and is about as far from good design as it could be. Visual effects should be essentially humorous – and if they make the garden feel a little bigger in the process then that's a bonus.

Mirrors

Mirrors are perhaps the widest and most easily used space enhancers, but need to be carefully sited to get the best effect. There is absolutely no point in positioning one at the end of a pergola or vista where you merrily see yourself coming down the garden path – the effect is immediately blown. The secret is

to place a mirror at an angle to a viewpoint so that the reflection takes in another part of the garden. If you have a tiny courtyard and you sit in a particular place then try positioning a mirror on one of the side walls or boundaries, inside a small archway. Place pots and planting to either side, carry the paving up to the mirror and the effect will be a way into an adjoining garden room. The first time round it really can fool you, after that you know what is going on, but the effect is fun and it does work. Some people worry that birds will fly into a mirror but, in my experience, if you partially cover it with planting or a tracery of branches there is little problem.

As far as quality is concerned, I often use recycled mirrors from old furniture. If the silvering breaks down slightly it really does not matter, as the reflection is naturally pretty confused by planting and other images.

False doors

Leading on from this effect, there is nothing wrong with a false door set against a wall, if you do it properly with a couple of steps in front, a pediment on top and a frame around the outside. Add a couple of urns or clipped box trees and train a wisteria over it. This will be a real focal point with a hint of something beyond. To be really clever, have the door slightly ajar and play around by angling a mirror in the gap.

Left While false doors and archways rarely fool anyone, they can certainly be fun, adding depth to the smallest gardens. Here pebbles, tiles and planting surround a mirror that seems to offer a glimpse of a garden beyond – it's actually rather fun!

Right There is real character to this old wooden door that naturally draws the eye and creates a focal point within a colourful mantle of bougainvillea.

Trompe l'oeil

False perspective, or to give it the proper name *trompe l'oeil*, can work well in certain situations but be careful: it can end up looking awfully pretentious.

In a small garden you can taper a lawn or long pool very slightly and this will certainly make the feature feel a little longer. Regularly placed pots or clipped trees can reinforce the perspective, especially if you reduce them in size with distance. Remember though that this effect will only work one way: when you reach the other end and look back the view is distinctly odd. I'll talk about lights and lighting techniques in more detail on pages 124–131, but one of my very favourite effects is to use points of light at diminishing distances. At night this is absolutely wonderful and creates enormous perspective. It works because the rest of the garden is difficult to see so you really don't know how long the space is. Most false perspective tricks look best in a formal design with one set of pots, lights or whatever you are using, arranged in symmetrical pairs.

Murals

Murals are yet another special effects technique and can add enormously to the charisma of a small space. They don't really fool anybody but are huge fun and can add a splash of colour and interest to bland or dominating walls.

In certain situations there is little or no room for planting, particularly in a town garden where the whole floor may be hard surfaced. Pots can brighten the scene but plants placed in them rarely grow very large. In this case a well-painted climber or complete border can change an outlook entirely, bringing a completely new dimension to the area. On a smaller scale, one or more windows painted onto a wall with an image of the sea, countryside or garden beyond will again do much to increase a feeling of space. Murals are traditionally a Mediterranean art form but there is absolutely no reason why they should not be more widely used, especially as they have the ability to cheer up the most dismal outlook.

Left Murals can transform an oppressive wall into a work of art and, as well as being attractive, can last indefinitely. Their pattern is only limited by the imagination of the creator, so make the most of them!

Right There are places where it is impossible to grow anything at all and, in this case, painted plants can be the answer. This larger-than-life Arum lily has great charm and not only brings life to a blank wall but leads the eye up the steps from one level to another.

Boundaries

While the house provides a natural link with the garden, don't forget the design cues that boundaries may offer. These usually run out from a building, often enclosing a simple rectangle or, particularly in an urban situation, at all kinds of angles and these can form the starting point for an underlying design pattern (see page 50). In small gardens, fences or walls may project to form bays, with all kinds of scope for built-in storage, a small shed, raised bed, barbecue or integrated seating. A bay could be a natural niche for a statue, water feature or other focal point. Don't overlook or screen the possibilities of an awkward corner or angle – it could be the start of something good.

You need to think about how the overall garden design can be worked to focus on what is a heaven-sent opportunity. Roof gardens have the greatest possibilities of all and here the treatment of boundaries is absolutely crucial to the finished composition. While shelter is often a requirement, so too is the view. You might lower a boundary, still providing safety and shelter but also to embrace a vista. Alternatively a wing of slatted fence, which is ideal to allow wind to filter through with minimum turbulence, can be just enough to screen a bad view and direct your line of sight in an altogether better direction.

Below There are situations where the erection of a boundary would be criminal. If you have a good view and are not over-looked, do away with the barrier altogether and enjoy the borrowed landscape.

The importance of materials

One important point I'd like to drop in here is how your choice of materials for a boundary or screen can change your perception of space.

Picture a room where the walls are papered with a bold, strongly coloured pattern. The effect is pretty obvious; the shapes catch the eye and demand attention. As a result the room feels smaller than if it were painted in a pastel shade. Take this analogy outside and you will find that a fence or screen of wide timber slats tends to foreshorten the space and bring the boundary in. Bold-leaved plants do exactly the same thing. If you have a relatively close boundary you should avoid both of these and instead use narrow slats and delicate planting. These tend to refract light and visually push the boundary away. Panels of vertically woven bamboo or reeds are excellent in this case and so too are grasses and plants with small or light foliage.

Left A rugged boundary of concrete blocks roughly rendered with a cement mortar has its own definite character. The ragged top sets up a rhythm while the seat is cantilevered out from the face. Galvanized buckets make sensible plant containers.

Right What else but a room with a view? This tiny garden is suspended over the street in a 'Mary Poppins' world of roofs, chimney pots and open sky. The actual sitting area may not be great but the feeling of space is enormous.

Removing boundaries

Before we move on from boundaries, I'd like to raise the possibility of doing away with them entirely. In most situations they serve a purpose, providing security, keeping children and pets in and unwanted things, including unsightly views, out. However, there are situations where you can remove part or all of a boundary with amazing results. Where there is a glimpse or the whole of a view beyond an unyielding fence, take out a section and let that view flow in, as long as security is not a problem. The result can be dramatic, increasing the visual dynamics of your plot enormously. I have done this in gardens on the edge of golf courses, seascapes and parks with great effect.

Framing a view

This same principle works at ground level. When designing a garden room with a view I'm often asked not to obstruct the latter in any way at all. A wide-open view is all well and good, but a focused one can be even better. It's like a painting which looks perfectly adequate on the canvas but is thrown into much sharper relief when surrounded by a frame. You have to choose carefully: the wrong frame can destroy the integrity of a painting or a view. It could be a wing of wall or fence to one side, smothered or fronted with planting. The wall might be scalloped down to allow the eye to drift into the view rather than abruptly stopping in a vertical line. In a formal garden the wall would be shaped down on either side of the view to form a balanced pattern. In an asymmetric composition there might be a well-detailed slatted fence as one side of the frame, a stand of small trees or shrubs to the other and a sweep of ground-covering plants between the two, balance being achieved with different weights and emphasis.

Wall space

Boundaries and walls are invaluable in a small garden and it's well worth remembering that their total surface area may be considerably more than the floor. In fact the smaller the garden, the greater, proportionally, the wall space. Not only will boundaries be vehicles for a potentially huge range of features and furnishings but, by their very size, they may present problems in the overall design of the garden. You may find you have one or more boundaries that soar above your outside room, particularly in an urban situation. These may provide a degree of privacy and shelter, but conversely could be full of overlooking windows or just be downright oppressive. Either way, they need turning to your advantage.

Overheads

One of the best ways to break an intrusive view from someone else's window is to use overhead beams that run out over your sitting space. These will not only ensure privacy but also act as a host for fragrant climbers to provide dappled shade in a sunny spot. Such a structure can be neatly fixed to the wall of a house and if made in timber could be painted to match woodwork elsewhere. As with a pergola, keep the detailing simple. All that fancy nosing off at the ends with odd scallops and angles is quite unnecessary. Keep timbers square and use generous dimensions and they will look just right; as before, let the plants be the stars.

Don't hang baskets from the beams. It clutters them up and you'll get a headache when you walk into them. Mind you, I have seen the sides screened off with glass bead curtains, which was charming and gave the effect of a casbah, particularly as the rest of the garden was furnished in much the same style.

Location has a lot to do with style. Outside a Mediterranean villa, the piers could be of simple brickwork with rustic poles carrying vines or other climbers. Other countries and architectural styles will suggest other treatments: just bear in mind the link between inside and out.

In many parts of the world verandahs do much the same job and form the perfect link between inside and out. Being roofed they provide shelter from sun and rain alike, but being open to the garden on the one hand and the building on the other gives a fluid transition between the two. Very often the flooring materials are the same, reinforcing the link. A raised verandah with broad steps dropping down to the garden not only gives you an excellent view but also a comfortable feeling of well being as you are slightly divorced from the wider environment.

Coming back to the wider, or higher, issue of walls dominating a garden as they soar above you, there is a useful trick that is well worth remembering. In such a situation I often define the vertical limit of the yard with overheads, or a similar structure. Then I paint everything below the overheads in a colour, usually a pale shade to maximize light in what can often be a shady spot. This has the instant effect of containing the view within the outside room: the overheads and perhaps even a

small tree providing a partial ceiling. Once you have set this upper limit, the walls above are far less noticeable and everything below can become part of a more intimate garden space. Overheads are not the only thing you can use; awnings provide a link with colour schemes inside the house and have the effect of filtering light into soft shade. You don't necessarily need an expensive canopy; a cotton throw tossed over a simple structure can look great and be just as effective.

Shelter

I'm forever reminding people that it is lack of shelter that can make living outside uncomfortable, whether this be from sun or a chill wind. Think of an al fresco restaurant that is so delightful in the summer with tables on the pavement. However, with the onset of autumn, blinds will be attached to the sides for protection and overhead heaters fitted so that dining can continue in the open for as long as possible. In a garden, one side of your overhead beams might be filled in with a low wall, say 1m (3ft 3in) high, with built-in seating and the space above fitted with vertical slats that carry a fragrant climber. In a wider garden a screen could be built out at right angles from a fence or boundary wall, again offering a place for a sheltered seat or larger sitting area. We enjoy living outside, so use these same techniques at home to prolong the pleasure – you might even save a little on restaurant bills.

Left Enclosure is the very stuff of all gardens and small gardens in particular. This yard is a clever study in horizontal and vertical geometry, with the clipped box hedges at ground level echoing the square-framed overhead beans that offer support to the wisteria. Vertical slats provide a delicate boundary linking upper and lower space.

Pool garden

For many years James Van Sweden and Wolfgang Oehme have ploughed their own distinctive furrow through the American garden scene, producing compositions that perfectly suit both the owners and the surrounding landscape. Here is the old truth that two heads can often be better than one and the combination of a strong underlying design structure linked to a sensitive planting scheme is hard to beat.

As in much contemporary design it is the architectural hard landscape framework that sets the theme and on this gently sloping site a series of terraces have been constructed that are linked by broad easy going steps. The focus of the area is the long pool which is both for swimming and simple visual delight. It is refreshing that more and more designers are realising that many features can have a dual or even multifunctional purpose and it need not be necessary to have the gaunt lines of a swimming pool set in stark contrast to the surrounding garden. Such an approach is even more valid where space is limited and anything that can subtly double up is of real value.

In this instance the change of level has been used to good advantage with the upper pool being given over to aquatic planting and being quite separate from the main area of water. The linking element is the simple but elegant bowl that spills water, pumped from below, in a generous cascade into the lower pool, providing both sound and movement, particularly welcome on a hot summer's day.

Left Water should always be used in a positive way and this simple yet elegant cascade, that sits on the broad stone coping, is the perfect link between the upper and lower pools.

Right There is a wonderful feeling of linearity in this design that leads your eye down the space and out into the lush planting at the far end. There is ample room for sitting while dappled sunlight, filtered through the trees makes this a warm and secluded corner.

Above Attention to detail is important in any garden and particularly in those elements that form the hard landscape structure. Notice how the coping over-hangs the walls so that the water can lap gently below it and how the light is recessed into the side of the steps to cast illumination exactly where needed.

A particularly pleasing aspect of the design is the way in which the various surfaces 'slide' over one another, the pool leading off into the planting at one end and the nearby steps dropping down to a far less controlled area of the composition where a path meanders through shrubs and perennials to terminate at a secluded garden house. Here is a complete change in mood that in turn allows this small area to feel rather larger than it actually is. These are those classic elements of mystery and surprise as the garden unfolds as you pass from place to place. Because of the different areas you tend to pause in each one and this is the perfect way in which to enjoy a small garden to the full.

Materials used for construction are simple and straightforward with natural stone walls capped with sawn stone to provide a crisp contrast. The paving, in simple square slabs, has been set at 45 degrees to the main garden grid and as a result provides a low key secondary pattern.

But it is the planting that really brings this small garden alive, both wrapping it in a protective cocoon to provide shelter and screening and softening the crisp architectural outline. There is no fussiness here though, species are chosen for their shape, texture and form so that they contrast one with another. Here, too, the principles of bold drifts and groups are used to the full with the true touch of a plantsman's eye.

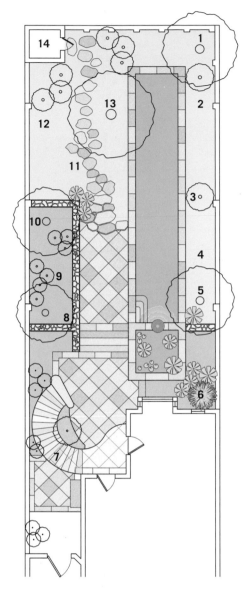

KEY

1 *Syringa reticulata*
2 *Chasmanthium latifolium*
3 *Hydrangea quercifolia* 'Snow Queen'
4 *Pennisetum alopecuroides*
5 Magnolia
6 Bamboo
7 Steps
8 Retaining walls
9 Mixed planting
10 *Cornus kousa*
11 Stepping stone path
12 Mixed planting
13 *Lagerstroemia indica*
14 Store

Above In this part of the garden the architectural pattern gives way to a far less formal approach. Here rough hewn stone steps give way to stepping stones that meander through softly modelled planting.

Left Here is the classic example of 'reversal' planting with one shape and form providing a positive contrast with its neighbour. Such planting is even more telling when worked against a simple plane of water that provides a non-demonstrative counterpoint.

Garden of Walls

Some gardens are delicate, sensual places, others have a wealth of complex planting, while still more have the ability to wrap you about in a safe and satisfying family environment. This garden is none of these. It is a strong and powerful statement that thrusts its character at you in a welter of colour, concrete and raw stone.

Here we are dealing with the positive expression of art and I find it so encouraging that designers are breaking down preconceived barriers and creating such rich and positive statements. This is a place that brings forth strong reactions by breaking many conventional perceptions. To me, deconstructivism is the taking apart of the latter and then reassembling these same components in a different pattern that positively challenges what is generally normal and acceptable.

But when we look at this space, it works well. There is ample room for all kinds of activities, the steps are broad and generous and the planting, although minimal, both softens and enhances the abrupt changes in level. In short, all the elements have been handled in an assured and positive manner. Where things become a little more challenging is in the wonderful handling of the poured concrete walls that rear out of the bed rock in a series of conflicting lines

Above This is pure sculpture with rock and concrete in perfect visual harmony. The deep shadow adds a feeling of mystery and no doubt a habitat for unexpected and varied wildlife, while the Pennisetums hang down from above.

Far left There is a fantastic dialogue here between the various garden elements. The rugged power of rock contrasts with the smooth concrete walls, while planting tumbles down the slopes like an approaching tsunami.

Left There is an honesty about concrete that makes it an indispensable material for so many situations. This is a straight-forward, no-nonsense flight of steps that sets itself apart from the other garden elements, allowing you to enter the space in a thoroughly purposeful way.

Above Beauty is ever in the eye of the beholder and this pattern is abstract art of the highest order. In a gallery it would be called an installation, but the truth is that many contemporary gardens are just that and the fact that one is inside and the other out matters little. The interest here lies in the beautiful three-dimensional interplay of surfaces.

and angles. Some of these follow the bedding plane of the rock below, others are tipped over, while some fold themselves around their rocky neighbours. There are all kinds of analogies here but the overall composition seems to mimic a jumbled series of fault lines where nature has pushed, pulled and wrenched the ground apart in an ever-changing pattern.

Colour is important in any situation and here it positively brings the concrete to life by using warm, earthy tones that are kept quite separate from the natural stone. This emphasizes the stone, giving it added power and stability.

To some the planting may seem insubstantial but in reality the aggressive shapes of the agave are the perfect adjunct to the smooth concrete walls. The Pennisetums, on the other hand, are far more delicate and in direct contrast to the other garden elements, having the ability to sway gently in the wind and soften the overall effect.

This is certainly not a garden for the fainthearted nor is it a place for the dedicated plantsperson, but what is does have in abundance is character and a sense of fun.

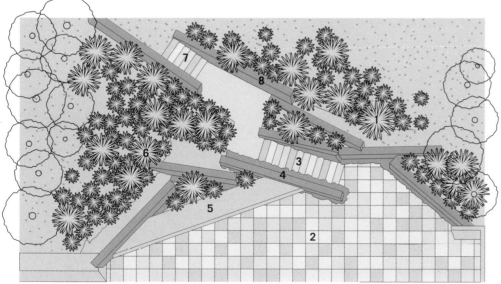

KEY
1 Planting of agave and pennisetum
2 Paving
3 Concrete steps
4 Coloured concrete walls built off
   natural stone
5 Concrete retaining walls/seat
6 Planting of agave and pennisetum
7 Concrete steps
8 Coloured concrete walls

3

STRUCTURE AND FORM

Choosing materials

More often than not, a small garden is a multifunctional space and has to include a wide range of features and furnishings. The danger – and the more limited the space, the more pertinent this is – is that the area can so easily become a mess.

By now you will have a good idea of the kind of garden you are going to create. You have been through the design process, decided on a theme and got the whole thing down on paper or in your mind. In all probability you will have been round myriad garden centres, visited shows and perhaps even created the wish list mentioned on page 16. It will have become clear from all of this just how vast the choice of building materials is. This is where many people go wrong – including good few designers too.

In your design there will be a natural split between the 'hard landscape' materials of paving, walling and associated features, and the 'soft landscape' of the planting. In sequential terms, and this is also an area that many people get back to front, the hard landscape forms the bones of the composition. The paved areas, paths, steps, walls and dividers create a framework into which the planting is placed. The latter softens and surrounds the garden, bringing it alive with colour and interest throughout the year. This is not a haphazard process and there should be a delicate balance between these two major elements. One of the best ways of achieving this is to select your hard landscape framework carefully, linking it to the styles of the house and the garden.

Below Such powerful lines of paving set up a definite rhythm with a strong directional emphasis. To counteract this, bold planting provides division and acts as 'punctuation marks' at the end of the various courses.

Above Any garden is a combination of hard and soft landscape, the former providing a frame for the latter. In a small space the two elements need careful juxtaposition. Here is a real synergy between the curved metal retaining walls, the purple fence, the gravels of different colours and the architectural planting.

Right Showering in the open air is hard to beat and the linking factor in this design is the use of slats for the decking, seat and fence. Planting scrambles up and through the latter while the surrounding trees draw the eye out of the garden, providing borrowed landscape.

Materials for boundaries

Your garden boundaries are probably already in place and you may have dreamed up all kinds of ways to enhance and improve them, or decided to leave things alone. However, one day you may need to replace them and this is a golden opportunity to improve on the original, both in terms of style and the materials used. For all practical purposes there are three broad types of boundary: walls, fences and hedges, each having their own characteristics.

Walls

Walls are durable and expensive, and are the kings of enclosure. They can extend the line of a building out into the garden with a feeling of continuity. If you are starting from scratch, it makes sense to respect the materials and style of architecture, matching a brick house with brick walls, a concrete-block house with block walls and timber house with neither of these but, you've guessed it, a fence.

Brick, well built and in good condition, is beautiful in its own right. I'm not starting a diatribe about damp-proof courses and copings, but a well-built wall should have both of these. A simple brick-on-edge coping is all you need:

Below Walls are often the best boundaries. A plain surface provides a clean line and a definite delineation of space that can be preferable to the embrace of climbing plants in a modern setting.

Left To pierce a wall and embrace a view can be wonderfully effective. Here the contrast between the cactus and the oval window is both dramatic and a real piece of landscape art. So often we think nothing of using strong colour inside the home but are timid in the garden, but perhaps you should think again when you see how eye-catching it can be.

Right The top, or coping, of a wall can make a great difference to the overall finish as well as offering protection from the elements. These overlapping tiles set up a very definite pattern, the colour linking with the granite setts used as paving below.

don't mess it up with fancy tile-creasing courses and the like, so much beloved by architects and engineers. If a brick wall is in bad condition you may be able to give it a new lease of life by applying a cement render to tie the whole thing together. Similarly a concrete block wall may benefit from the same treatment. Then you will have a smooth surface just right for colour washing, which should get you thinking about linking with a scheme inside the house. If you have wide glass sliding doors, simply continue a wall colour from inside to out. Group plants in big pots outside and house plants on the inside and you will really minimize the transition between the two living spaces.

Lighting can play a role here too. Uplighters placed against the inside wall can be continued outside to draw you into the garden on a warm evening.

Except perhaps in a hi-tech modern garden, walls call out for plants and climbers. Never put trellis on walls. It simply breaks the continuity and line of the background and creates a maintenance problem, particularly when fully clothed with a rampant climber. It is far better simply to wire the wall with horizontal strands spaced vertically about 45cm (18in) apart and tie the climbers to these. Should you want to paint or repair the surface at any time, it is easy enough to detach the wires, lay them and the planting on the ground.

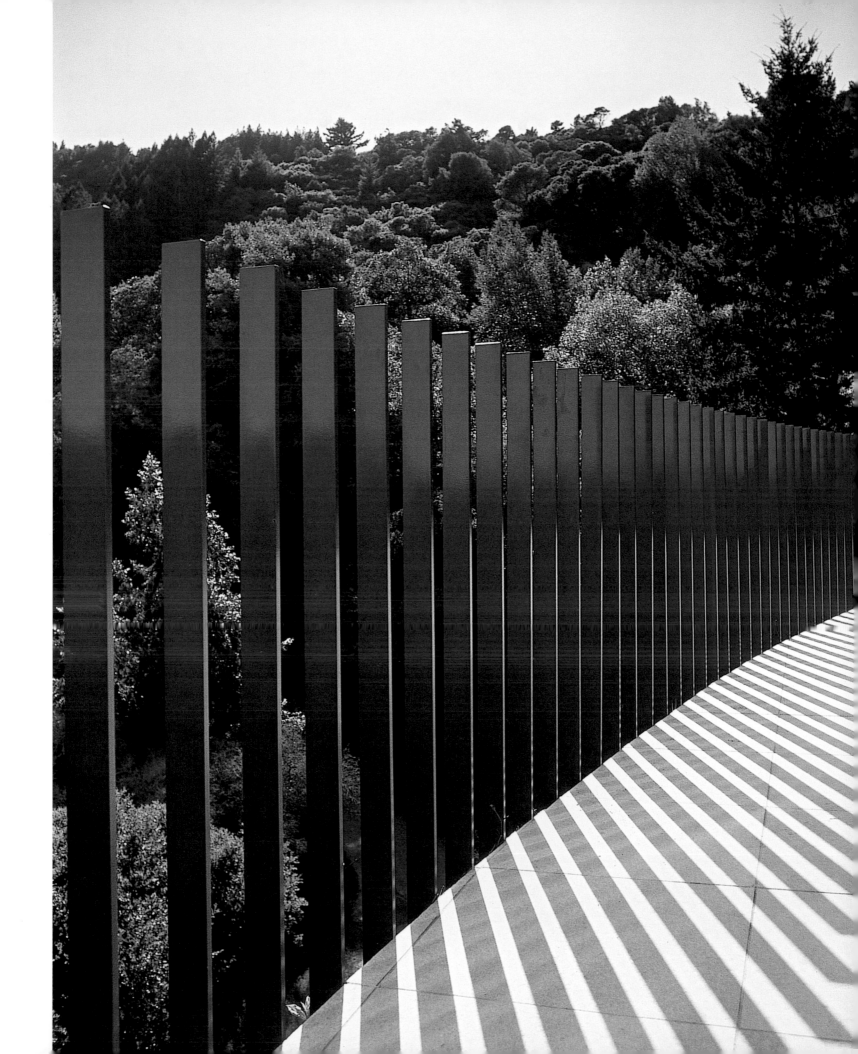

Fences

Fences are far cheaper than walls but do not last as long. Think about the style and don't put up the first off-the-peg panels you see at your nearest home improvement store. Like a wall, a good fence has the ability to link strongly with the adjoining building. The line and method of construction are important. Broad horizontal boards, often called 'ranch fencing', tend to accelerate the view and your eye travels quickly down their length. This can be a good or bad thing, depending on the design and situation of the garden. Vertical boards have the effect of slowing things down a little. Varying the widths of boards or slats will set up their own rhythms. Another idea is to vary the height of the slats, so the top of the fence has an irregular outline. This can look brilliant in an integrated fencing and boundary design where the structures positively relate to one another but, if done without sensitivity, could look a contrived mess.

There is a fad at the moment to paint fences and walls all kinds of fancy colours. Don't – unless you have a really good reason for doing so. As soon as you introduce a colour scheme, it poses problems when choosing and using plants. A straightforward brown is a natural landscape colour that relates to most things around it. In this case, simple things work best.

Neither do I like convoluted hand-made trellising that costs a fortune. It may look fine in a catalogue and even prettier at a garden show but will almost certainly look pretentious in your own back yard. Remember, the plants are the stars: the vehicle should be a simple, strong and low-key background.

If you really want to go out on a limb, think laterally. In a very modern garden I have made screens using heavy-duty coloured plastic mesh. It is an excellent host for climbers which quickly scramble over the surface – just be careful about choosing which colour climber. I have also used translucent woven polyester for fencing, stretched between aluminium posts. The result was extremely practical, filtering the wind, casting little shadow and being surprisingly durable. Its weight, too, was a terrific advantage: you could roll up a 10m (33ft) run, including the posts, and put it over your shoulder. The drawback, however, is that climbers cannot cling to the surface.

Scaffold poles set in concrete make efficient screens. Painted black they become almost invisible, allowing twining climbers to be shown off to great advantage. This question of colour is an important one: black absorbs light and is difficult to see; white, on the other hand, reflects light and becomes very obvious. This is the reason why white trellis stands out so clearly, which is not always something that you want in a garden.

Above Timber poles, if treated against rot, can form a durable and no-nonsense boundary, looking particularly effective set against a woodland background.

Left A fence is simply a barrier to the outside world and if spaced slats are used, the view can flow into the garden. Shadow is an ever-useful design tool and here casts an attractive secondary pattern onto the floor.

Hedges

In this increasingly instant world we tend to forget about materials that take a while to establish, but hedges can create an exceedingly fine boundary. They do need some time to grow and a degree of maintenance along the way but, once mature, they provide a unique blend between architectural form and the softness of neighbouring planting.

Below A low wall can often be backed by a tall hedge to provide shelter and privacy. In this small garden there is an interesting contrast between the strong horizontal line of the wall and the verticality of the bamboo stems that becomes a design statement in its own right.

There is a misconception that certain species of hedge are particularly slow to develop. While this is true up to a point, the real secret to planting anything is good preparation. I grow yew hedges in my own garden and they are generally considered to be the slowest of all. With a degree of hard work when I planted them, including preparing a deep hand-dug trench with a good mix of top soil and manure, the end result is spectacular. They have grown between 15–23cm (6–9in) each year and are now a respectable 2m (6ft 6in) high.

Hedges can be broadly divided into two categories: closely clipped and informal.

The first type are just what they say and make excellent boundaries or internal screens. If well grown and correctly clipped they will be virtually impenetrable and good for security, species with thorns or spines particularly so.

Some of the faster-growing species such as conifers or privet can present problems, as they extract a huge amount of moisture and goodness from the ground. This can make it difficult to grow other more decorative planting nearby. However, with regular feeding and watering these difficulties can be largely overcome. I'll be talking about plant selection later, but the secret to planting anything successfully is to understand its characteristics. Vigorous species grow fast and high, and need a regular and sometimes ruthless maintenance programme to keep them looking at their best. When clipping any hedge, always taper the profile so that it is slightly narrower at the top than the bottom.

Another advantage of hedging is its malleability: you can clip it straight along the top, castellate it,

introduce curves or swoop it up and down. Think of the ways in which it could link with the overall garden design. This is verging on the art of topiary and there is absolutely no reason why you should not include one or more shapes, figures or animals, provided that they are part of the overall garden theme.

Informal hedges are rather different and by their very nature take up more space, something that is not always practical in the smallest of gardens. Space will depend on the species selected; while a sprawling rose hedge grows high and wide, shrubs like potentilla, lavender, deutzia and spirea make attractive small-scale dividers rather than boundaries.

Fruit trees trained as cordons or espaliers can create ideal internal divisions within the garden, perhaps between decorative and vegetable or utility areas. Alternatively, use them simply for the joy of seeing their blossom and eating their fruit.

One final yet important point before we leave the subject of boundaries. There is little point in buying or designing something if it is not installed correctly, a fact that applies to most things inside and outside the home. In a garden wear and tear can be considerable, so don't skimp on the techniques or the materials used for construction. Fences and screens need firm fixings, concreted into the ground or securely bolted to an adjoining building or wall.

Left Hedges offer a softer garden boundary than either walls or fences and here there is a real feeling of perspective that draws your eye down to the classic stone urn carefully positioned as the focal point at the end of the path. The purple-leaved beech offers an attractive colour contrast with the variegated *Lamium* that provides low-maintenance ground cover at the base of the hedge.

Taking your cue from the house

In architecture, as in most forms of design, less is more. By this I mean that constraint in choosing and using materials is almost invariably a good thing. Overcomplication and busy patterns rarely bring an atmosphere of tranquillity – an important factor in a garden.

When looking for a suitable exterior floor, a good starting point is to take a cue from the house, either the surfaces used inside or the materials used for construction.

In an ideal situation an interior floor can simply be continued outside. Slate, stone or terracotta tiles look as handsome outside as in and naturally provide a seamless transition with little or no visual interruption. There may need to be a slight change in level to prevent water or damp penetrating the building but the visual theory is a sound one. Timber is another natural choice: floorboards can easily and subtly become a deck. The real trick is to respect the direction and line of surfaces. Where a particular paving pattern or grid is used inside, continue the same pattern on the other side of the threshold. So often you see boards or paving well used but the joints don't line up. There is nothing more frustrating to a sensitive eye. Even worse is to change the pattern entirely: boards that run towards glass doors should continue in the same line outside, sweeping the eye into the garden and towards some kind of view or focal point. All too often an insensitive builder – or, even worse, an architect – turns them at right angles on the deck, completely destroying any continuity.

Even with carpet or other kinds of floor coverings there is often scope for linkage. I have designed carpets with a linear pattern and repeated that same pattern or colour as paving in the garden. The same can be done with vinyl or composite floorings; the real point is an awareness of moving from inside to out and reinforcing this link wherever possible.

Occasionally you can do something special. I have worked on schemes where a pool inside can be either physically linked to one outside or divided by only the narrowest margin. Changes in level can be exploited, with water channelled across a verandah, then tumbling into a pool below. Modern, and sometimes not so modern, architecture is a rich catalyst in such thinking – keep your eyes open and remember details to re-use elsewhere.

Below A strong link with the house can make a small garden feel larger, allowing interior and exterior space to flow together. Here this is encouraged by glass sliding doors and similar flooring inside and out.

Neither paving or other surfaces need necessarily be linked at ground level. For instance, a worktop from a kitchen can pass through a glass panel and continue outside to house a barbecue. In the smallest of gardens this could be turned to real advantage, with built-in seating, raised beds and planting completing the overall picture.

Where there is no obvious design cue to be picked up from rooms within the home, you may need to look to the façade of the building itself for inspiration. As I discussed with boundaries on page 90, the link may well be a natural one. A stone-built house may suggest stone paving or walls, brick with brick, concrete with concrete, while timber cladding could provide the necessary cue for a well-detailed wooden deck or fence.

Above This little yard flows out from the building with serpentine beds edged with steel and planted with bamboo and box. The metal mesh flooring provides another material link with the adjoining architecture.

Garden floors

The problem with paving and other kinds of surfacing is the vast choice available. Take a trip to any garden centre or home improvement store and you'll see what I mean. While this is not necessarily a bad thing, it can cloud the issue and is something to bear in mind when dealing with what is quite likely to be the largest section of your overall budget. Your design will have determined the outline and extent of any paved areas. You may have thought about what materials you might use, particularly if you have been building up a mood board or collecting tear sheets of various ideas you have seen and liked. Before thinking of paving, decking, gravel or any other hard surface, don't ignore grass or another plant surface as a major element within the composition.

Below Floors need not be 'hard' and plants, including grass, can provide a wonderful surface. Broad sweeps and drifts create a sense of space and movement, leading both feet and eye through a space.

Grass and lawns

There is the argument that in a tiny space grass becomes impractical, simply because it gets worn out by feet, pets and ball games. However, in many situations, wear may not be high and the softening influence of a lawn can be perfect in an otherwise unyielding environment. Providing there is ample light and the garden is not overshadowed, grass can bring a touch of the countryside into the most urban patch. I have designed many tiny gardens for folk who have moved down from a large plot where they had spent many a happy hour mowing and edging. There is something rewarding, not to say mindless, about tending a lawn. You can switch off from the mundane pressures of life by becoming involved in a straightforward manual job.

In a small garden the shape of a lawn should be simple: convoluted curves and awkward angles are not easy to maintain. If grass adjoins a higher surface such as a raised bed or steps, build in a simple mowing edge that can take the form of a row of bricks or paving slabs. The turf should be laid slightly higher than the hard surface so that a mower can run smoothly over the top. Grass seed mixtures can be varied for different situations, such as shady spots or areas where wear and tear is higher. A good landscape contractor can advise on this.

Ground-cover plants

Apart from grass there are other options that you might find attractive in certain areas. Many ground-covering plants will form an elegant and relatively durable floor. Sweeps of thyme will be gloriously colourful and fragrant in a sun-soaked courtyard, either planted in a bed or within areas of paving where they can spread and self-seed endlessly. In shadier places that versatile and useful plant *Alchemilla mollis* is indispensable for colonizing nooks, crannies or larger areas, as is *Helxine* (or *Soleirolia*) or my particular favourite, *Acaena*. The latter hail from New Zealand, they hug the ground with tiny leaves and bronze-coloured burr-like seed heads. Look closely at them and you will see a miracle of nature – delicate in form but physically tough, making them useful in many situations.

Many garden owners who subsequently become gardeners learn in time not to be over-zealous. It's a simple thing; to pull out every self-seeded plant that finds itself a home in your garden is horticultural murder. These colonizers add immeasurably to your yard, so learn to enjoy them for what they are and what they can achieve.

Above The warm, gentle colour of these rooftop sedums blend well with the small cobbles and clean lines of the decking, the slatted wooden seat cleverly continuing the lines of the latter.

Combining flooring materials

In most situations doors from the house give way to a paved area. In a very small garden this could comprise virtually the whole outside space. While the adage less is more still holds true, there is a degree of sensible compromise here and, as a general rule, a single paving material can become visually a little heavy or bland. Conversely three or more are likely to look too busy. Logic suggests that two surfaces could be good, with one of these being the dominant partner. In a brick-built house, a grid of brickwork at ground level could extend outwards to form a natural visual link, the grid being filled in with another kind of paving. In a crisp architectural situation this might be a regular pattern of pre-cast concrete slabs of a similar size; in a less formal situation you could use random flags of a natural stone. The grid would hold both together and link with the building. Alternatively you might make a paved terrace but omit a number of slabs, filling the gaps with panels of brick. This would be a less geometric approach, but would have the same effect of one surface softening the other and forming a bond with the adjoining building.

Remember that paving is usually a background and should be low key. Slabs should not be brightly coloured – they will not only look ostentatious but fade to even more sickly hues. Similarly, broken or 'crazy' paving has an inherently busy outline and does not sit comfortably close to the cleaner lines of a building. You can minimize this by laying it in panels contained within a grid of another material but, as a general rule, it is better used in informal situations in a larger garden.

Opposite In a traditional garden stone adds a feeling of stability and permanence. These small cobbles, precisely laid in a contrasting fan pattern, naturally lead you out into this small courtyard that is surrounded by clipped box balls and soft fern fronds.

Left Where there is access in and out of a house or garden there are natural routes called 'desire lines'. Here this is highlighted by a metal grid path laid though grey gravel, a subtle and crisp change of texture rather than colour.

Below Many people are horrified by the mere thought of using artificial grass in a garden but if you simply think of it as exterior carpet then the philosophy subtly changes. Being so light, it is ideal for roof gardens and can be precisely cut to complement other materials.

Using texture

Not only is texture a useful design tool in helping to contrast various surfaces, it also determines the speed at which you move around the place. Smooth paving encourages rapid movement, ideal for paths and well-trodden spaces. It also allows tables and chairs to be positioned without wobbling. Riven stone and many types of brick are slightly uneven, slowing you down slightly, which is often a good thing in a small garden. Solid cubes of granite or setts are even more uneven, while gravels and loose cobbles slow you down further.

At the top of the scale smooth boulders, which have such an architectural quality particularly when associated with planting, will stop you dead in your tracks. They can be useful in a front yard where delivery and other people regularly cross the space by taking a short cut across the garden. Boulders will divert both eye and feet in a particular direction, guiding them carefully around choice planting or perhaps a water feature. They can be used as design tools to create a greater feeling of space by leading you over a greater distance that takes just that little bit longer to walk, providing incidental interest along the way.

There is nothing new in this. The great landscaper Capability Brown did exactly the same things in a grand way with trees and contoured ground; we are simply doing it here on a smaller scale.

Above left Mirrored metal steps provide a visual double take in this gravel garden. While this is full of reflective fun you would need to watch your step to avoid a tumble into the *Carex*, something to bear in mind when using unusual materials and ideas.

Above right Much good garden design is to do with weaving different textures into a composition, both in terms of hard and soft landscape. In this rill there are subtle contrasts between water, smooth cobbles and the creeping ground cover 'Mind your own business', *Soleirolia soleirolii*.

Opposite When working with different levels it can be useful to indicate a step with a change of material. This defines separate areas and adds interest, preventing the scheme becoming visually heavy. This step is cleanly detailed, linking the raised beds.

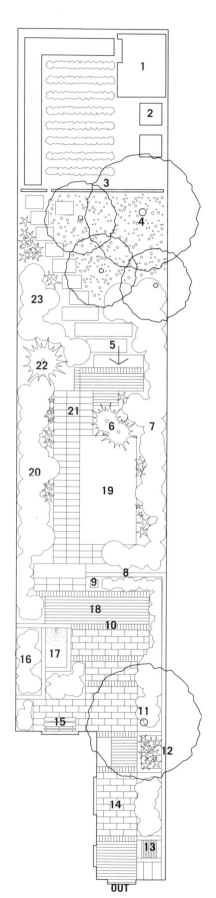

Directional emphasis

There is more to choosing and using a flooring material than just slapping it down on the ground. Its shape, size and the pattern in which it is laid may also have a considerable impact in visual terms. The smaller the garden, the more critical these factors are: employed intelligently they can be very useful design tools indeed.

In that long narrow garden of mine I mentioned earlier (see page 52 and diagram left), I did all the right things. I divided up the space with walls and planting, pushed the steps and paths to one side and then the other, and created different rooms – in short, it worked well. Lying around the house when we first moved in was a large pile of old blue bricks: they are not only indestructible and ideal for paths and walls, but were a perfect colour match for the roof slates. As a counterpoint to the bricks I used pale honey-coloured pre-cast concrete paving slabs, measuring 60 x 30cm (2 x 1ft) – the colour contrast was very effective.

To increase the width of this narrow yard I chose to lay courses of blue brick across the space. Between each band I then laid several rows of paving slabs in a stretcher bond, like bricks in a wall. By doing this I increased the visual width of the space because the pattern pushed out sideways. If I had laid the brick courses and slabs down the garden, I would have achieved the opposite effect and the garden would have appeared narrower. Think about a tall man in a pin-stripe suit: it emphasizes his height. Conversely, a pullover with broad bands around it makes the wearer look rather more ample in girth. All these design rules and guidelines work in whatever field you care to apply them.

KEY
1 Shed
2 Compost
3 Screen with climbers
4 Fruit trees in area of rougher grass naturalized with bulbs
5 Steps
6 Existing conifers
7 Mixed planting
8 Wall 1.8m (6ft) high
9 Statue
10 Courses of brick
11 Holly tree
12 Raised bed
13 Barbecue
14 Pre-cast concrete paving
15 Seat
16 Raised bed
17 Raised pool
18 Brick paving
19 Lawn
20 Mixed planting
21 Path
22 Existing conifer
23 Mixed planting

Laying patterns

Square slabs or tiles in a simple grid make a relatively static pattern but as soon as you overlap them, a degree of directional emphasis comes into play. Similarly with a brick path, if it is laid with a stretcher bond running down the path then your eye naturally follows and you walk that little bit faster. If these same bricks are laid in a pattern across the path then you slow down slightly. A bond such as basket weave that has two bricks turned one way and two the other is visually static, while herringbone, where bricks are laid diagonally, provides a feeling of fluid movement. All over Europe you see granite setts laid in those intricate fan patterns, which have a wonderful

Above A boardwalk encourages faster movement, but to counteract this the sharp turn will naturally slow you down. Such a device can be used to position a focal point that can be enjoyed before moving on to another part of the garden.

Right Just how you lay a path has a real impact on the speed you walk down it. In this traditional country garden setting a combination of old bricks, cobbles and clumps of thyme make for a casual stroll rather than a brisk walk. This in turn allows you to appreciate the immediate garden and planting to either side. Such a composition is to be appreciated in detail rather than summarily dismissed.

Left In this garden I used several 'tricks of the trade'. The slabs and bricks are laid across the garden to increase visual width, the main path leads down one side rather than the middle, and the whole space is divided into a series of separate rooms, each with their own theme. Although architectural and geometric, the end result is softened by generous planting.

rhythm that is far more interesting than simply laying them in straight lines.

In other words, apart from the inherent characteristic of a material, which you may choose to complement the house or provide a specific link with the rooms inside, you can also help manipulate the garden by using pattern in any number of different ways.

Laying techniques

Any surface needs to be bedded on mortar over good foundations of crushed stone or hardcore to prevent subsequent movement. Uneven surfaces are both unsightly and dangerous. It is important to spend a little more time and a sensible part of your budget getting this fundamental stage right: the job should only need doing once. The finished level should also be 150mm (6in) below any damp-proof course or membrane incorporated within the house walls.

Hard surfaces should also shed water easily, so paving should be sloped gently away from the building into drains or a planted area.

Materials for floors

The floor will often form the real backbone of your garden, dividing the spaces, defining the planted areas and, of course, allowing you access and ample room for sitting, dining, entertaining, play and many other essential functions.

Paving

Durability and suitability for a location also need to be taken into account when choosing paving. Paving of all kinds is naturally hard wearing, but the choices are legion. 'Natural' materials tend to be more expensive than man made and there is nothing to beat old flagstones outside a period property or crisply sawn slate or sandstone fronting a more modern façade. Such stone will last several lifetimes if properly laid. The slight variation in colour and surface texture with these material is always attractive.

Having said that, there has been a huge improvement in simulated paving made from concrete and all but the most discerning would have problems in distinguishing them from the real thing. The slabs have often been created from moulds cast from natural stone but the products almost invariably lack the subtle variations of the real thing. Costs, however, can be far lower, something that may well need taking into account.

There are also many slabs that have a plain, simple and no-nonsense finish in a wide range of sizes and can be laid to create all kinds of different patterns and directional emphasis (see diagram on page 104). Remember, it is more expensive to have a contractor lay small materials such as bricks, tiles or small slabs than larger slabs. The labour factor in laying small materials is higher.

Above There is something satisfying about precise geometry and this pattern has a great stability. The broad steps, flanked by planters, drop to the crisp grid of paving while square pots add their own rhythm in front of the bed. The neatly recessed lights cast illumination just where it is needed.

Right Natural materials such as gravel provide an interesting texture and also have the ability either to reflect light if pale in colour or to absorb it if darker – a useful design tool in high or low light levels.

Concrete

From a personal point of view I prefer to use concrete for what it is, the stone of the twentieth and twenty-first centuries. In many parts of the world it is an accepted landscape material, reasonable in cost, available in a wide range of finishes and ever flexible. By this I mean that it can be cast on site in panels or freeform shapes and also be mixed with different aggregates to provide a wide range of surface textures. For example, in 'brushed aggregate', the surface is carefully washed and brushed down just before it sets hard to expose the small stones in the mix. This ability to change the texture and colour of the material can be useful in a small, dark urban garden where pale aggregates can help to reflect light.

Tiles

Tiles of all kinds can be ideal in a garden and if used both inside and out, provide a natural link with the house. Materials such as terracotta have a warm Mediterranean feel; handmade versions that have a slight difference in size and texture gives them great character as well as a tactile quality. They would set up a delightful dialogue with pots made from a similar material, as well as adjoining colour-washed walls. Not all tiles will be well fired enough to withstand the frosts of a cold climate, so check with your supplier before buying.

I know one tiny garden where the creator, a talented artist, has taken a Moroccan theme and used brightly coloured tiles, deep blue walls, glass bead dividers and an eclectic collection of pots to create a composition of enormous character. Old walls soar around the space and for all intents and purposes you could easily be in North Africa, such is the power of the theme. The secret of this and many other gardens is in the detail. Materials chosen carefully and with sensitivity add immeasurably to the effect, but if used at random, with little thought to the finished picture, the area can easily become a mess. The dividing line is a narrow one – the difference between good and indifferent design.

Above Concrete is perhaps the most versatile material at our disposal. It can be cast or laid to virtually any pattern and works in any situation. The stepping stone that crosses this narrow pool matches the colour and texture of the adjoining paving perfectly, providing a straightforward understatement that is all that is necessary in such a situation.

Left Terracotta tiles bring visual warmth and a Mediterranean atmosphere to a garden. Here they have been set at an angle to the boundaries and the resulting diagonal lines increase the perceived space in this garden designed for outdoor living and relaxing.

Slate

Slate is a natural stone that can be used in all kinds of different ways. It can be 'riven' or split so that it has a slightly textured surface, sawn and polished into smooth slabs with an almost mirror-like surface, or rough hewn into large pieces that can stand alone in the garden as pure sculpture. If polished, slate can be slippery underfoot when wet, but for pure elegance, perhaps linking with a similar floor inside the house, it is hard to beat. Being almost black, it warms up quickly in sunlight and in hot countries can scorch bare feet. Because of its colour, it has the ability to set up stunning contrasts, particularly when used alongside a pale paving, concrete or range of gravels.

Cobbles, chippings and gravel

Coming down the size scale even further, we now have a vast range of stone cobbles, chippings and gravels at our disposal. These, too, can be really useful in reflecting light: pale chips can positively dispel the gloom of a dark, enclosed courtyard. Being loose they can be laid in complex patterns and shapes, as well as filling awkward corners where paving slabs would be difficult to cut in. Laid over a firm base they can form paths and hardstanding areas; in conjunction with planting, loose cobbles and chippings can be used as a mulch or ground cover, retaining moisture and helping to reduce weed growth. Gravel may need to be raked from time to time to restore its smooth appearance and to prevent it being trodden away from areas of heavier traffic. The only disadvantage of these materials is that they are not very comfortable if you like to be barefoot in the garden.

Much of the skill in using all these different hard landscape materials lies in understanding their inherent characteristics and how one can relate to another. Visiting other gardens and landscape situations helps this process enormously; always take a camera and notebook to record ideas and designs.

Above To use natural materials well needs a sympathetic understanding of their characteristics. The Japanese have been masters of the technique for many centuries. Here there is a strong influence from that country in the positioning of the slate step and vertically set slate tiles. Notice how the change of material from the gravel pathway indicates the step to come, while the posts to either side create a tension point as you enter the next garden room.

Left Laid in mortar and packed together as tightly as possible, cobbles can create all kinds of fascinating patterns. Here stones of different sizes and colours have been set in a meandering spiral, interspersed with glass marbles that sparkle in the sunlight, adding yet another element of interest to the floor.

Decking and timber

In some parts of the world decking has become something of a cliché, much overused and misunderstood. In reality it is the most useful of surfaces in a small area. One of its great advantages is ease of construction. Decks can be a real asset in covering unsightly paved or concrete areas, provided you can rationalize levels adjoining the house.

The secret of any deck lies in good ventilation below the surface. Boards should be laid on a framework of bearers or 'joists' to allow free circulation of air and drainage in wet weather.

In visual and spatial terms a deck can set up all kinds of sight lines and patterns. I have already mentioned the visual link of boards running from inside to out (see page 96), but deck boards can also be turned at an angle to the house so that they lead the eye in another direction, perhaps towards a specific focal point in another part of the garden. I often vary the widths of the boards to set up a fascinating rhythm. You can buy or build decking panels that can be turned at right angles to one another to set up yet another pattern. But whatever style you use, try to relate this to the overall design of the garden and don't allow yourself to get carried away by the versatility of the material itself.

Sloping gardens offer huge potential here. One deck can be carried out over a change of level and link with another that is lower or higher. Existing planting and trees can be allowed to grow through the deck (see page 18) and a natural interface exists between trees and a timber surface.

Boards are easily cut and shaped and can be fitted in awkward corners. Additionally, a deck can easily accommodate a hot-tub or other feature, while timber stains now available in a wide range of colours offer enormous potential. On a roof garden where excess weight can often be a major problem, decking provides a light and elegant surface that can be positioned over bearers to allow the necessary drainage.

As a final point, timber is a 'warm' material – a real asset when walking or basking on the surface.

Railway sleepers and other timber

Decks need suspending above a surface but you can use timber in the form of railway sleepers or ties as paving in its own right, bedded directly onto a suitable base. There

Below Timber is easily shaped and as such can conform to virtually any pattern. These serpentine boards demonstrate beautifully that decking need not run in straight lines. They are also lightweight and therefore perfect for this tiny roof garden, warm underfoot, tone down bright light and provide an excellent foil to the surrounding planting.

is something solid and satisfying in such a surface, while its dark colour and large size can be teamed with contrasting materials such as pale gravel and chippings to great effect. Because sleepers are long in relation to their width they can, like decking, be used to provide directional emphasis. Straight lines or at right angles to one another are simplest designs – they do not curve easily! Sleepers are available from various outlets: before buying check that they are clean and free from oil, which can sweat out in hot weather with dire consequences, particularly if you have a pale coloured carpet.

New sleepers, or at least timbers cut to similar dimensions, are now available and can look superb with their crisply sawn edges and grained surface. Used sensitively and in conjunction with many other kinds of paving they have all kinds of possibilities. Because of their weight they make superb steps or raised beds and can extend the line of similar materials used elsewhere in the scheme.

Throughout this book I am trying to encourage you to think laterally and explore the different ways you can use design, materials and plants to best advantage. A typical example would be to use sleepers or long balks of timber set vertically into the ground to form a sculpture. The heights could be varied and combined with architectural planting, smooth boulders and perhaps a simple plane of water for a very elegant result. Alternatively, timbers could be cut down into shorter lengths and bedded vertically in a trench to form a raised bed or simple retaining wall. Again, the height of the tops could be varied slightly to set up an interesting rhythm, with plants tumbling down to enhance and soften the outline. I would personally far rather use timber in this way than the ubiquitous round stakes that inevitably look flimsier and are busier on the eye. As in so much design, simple things work best, as well as usually lasting a good deal longer.

The range of materials at your disposal is legion and although I have covered the more accessible ones here, you will come across more. Whatever materials you choose, use them with sensitivity and with regard to their inherent characteristics and that of the area into which they will be incorporated.

Left Here there is extraordinary power in the relationship of the building, pool and deck, the latter being of ample size and laid in a chequerboard pattern that picks up on the adjoining façade.

Alternative materials

Garden design, like any art form, is moving on apace. Designers, myself included, are experimenting with materials of all kinds. Many of these are commonly used in other areas of design or industry but there has been considerable resistance to introducing them into the garden. I'm not saying that you have to use any of these, but you can create great originality and not a little humour if you do.

A few years ago, at an international garden show, I designed a large garden with a descending row of painted red rocks, together with planting, swirling shapes of gravel, glass and water. The effect was stunning and stimulating but set the cat amongst the horticultural pigeons in an unexpected way. All of the materials used were common enough but until that time had rarely cropped up in a garden, and I received both brickbats and praise in roughly equal proportions. I mention this to underline the point that we can tend to be terribly parochial in our exterior design outlook — we all need to loosen up a bit in our thinking.

Glass

If you have a modern bent, start to explore the rich palette of materials available. Glass is becoming increasingly popular: I love those richly coloured beads used by florists in the bottom of flower vases. They look like translucent sweets and, when the sun strikes them, they become alive with sparkling shafts of light. To be really effective in a garden they can be used as a 'marble' lawn or as a mulch between plants. A dry 'stream' of ruby or blue beads is breathtaking and they also work particularly well with water playing over the surface. Crushed glass is another similar option but this can sometimes have rough edges that could present a potential hazard underfoot in the wrong setting.

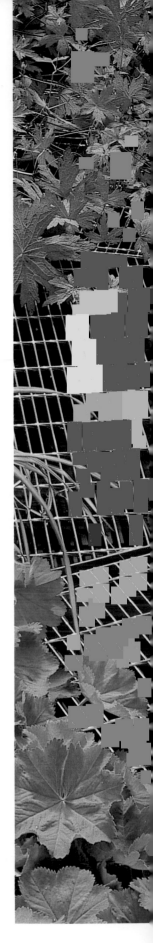

Left For far too long many designers have fought shy of using everyday materials in their work. Although not a traditional garden material, marbles in all kinds of colours can be used to form striking mulches and ground cover that sparkle in sunlight and glisten in the rain, bringing a whole new dimension of light and colour to the garden.

Right Metal mesh makes great paving: it is tough, allows drainage and can be used to set up all kinds of interesting patterns. Such a geometric and visually hard surface benefits from soft planting, the *Alchemilla*, *Carex* and geranium providing the perfect foil.

Metal

Galvanized buckets and containers have been widely used by florists for many years but are now finding their way into the garden. Metal is most definitely 'in' and, used in the right way and in the right setting, looks great. Containers of all kinds are now commonplace and from a horticultural point of view, the bigger the better to ensure an ample root run. When using this kind of material, think how it can relate to the rest of the scheme; in other words design the garden in the round, thinking about all the components and how they sit one with another.

I am fond of polished stainless steel and mirrored acrylic, where the reflected images of planting are given a new dimension. There are some breathtaking stainless-steel water features that would form a brilliant focal point in the smallest garden. To see what's available go to big garden shows, which are a veritable ideas factory of anything to do with the garden.

Plastics

Of all the materials with potential, plastics have been the slowest to emerge as a viable garden element. In a modern setting I find this difficult to understand. For example, industrial flooring is available in a huge range of colours, is often textured to ensure good grip underfoot and is resistant to virtually anything you can throw at it. If you simply think of it as a floor covering but used outside, it may be easier to overcome the psychological barrier. Think of the advantages of moulding a sloping garden into a series of fluid level changes using swirls of flooring laid over a concrete screed. Steps become redundant, children fly about, the surface is warm and relatively soft underfoot. Vinyl, rubberized or plastic coverings are vastly lighter than conventional paving and often cost less.

Plastic grass, commonly called Astroturf, has been around for years. Resistance to using it has been largely due to the fact that it imitates grass, even if it comes in a whole range of colours apart from green. But if you look on it as an outdoor carpet – which, of course, it is – then preconceptions largely disappear and it can offer a lightweight, durable and non-mow surface, ideal in situations where a lack of water and load bearing are an issue (see page 101 for an example of how good it can look).

Right Like marbles, crushed seashells, in this case dyed glorious shades of blue, provide a wonderful alternative ground cover and mulch. The rhythmic planting of small, low-growing clumps of *Leucogenes grandiceps*, which will eventually increase to form a carpet, is of a sufficiently different texture to contrast well with the undemonstrative background.

Water features

I have already touched on water features at various times during this book because I like to consider them in the context of what is under discussion at the time. In a small garden they are relatively straightforward, but it is worth seeing how the majority of them work and how they are fitted. Except in unusual circumstances, you will not be incorporating a large pond into your back yard, but smaller pools and cascades can be just right. As far as the construction is concerned, the smaller the pool, the neater this needs to be.

Pool 'liners' that are made from rubber or laminated plastics need to be well fitted and if possible concealed behind the brick or block work that forms the shell of the feature. It is possible to have liners tailor-made so that they neatly slot into place without puckering at the corners – inevitable when using a flat sheet. While concrete has been largely superseded as a constructional

Below This sculpted stone bowl is set over a tank fitted with a submersible pump. Water is pumped into the bowl through a seal at the base and cascades over the top through the bed of cobbles into the tank.

material for big pools, mainly because of its tendency to form hair-line cracks, it is often still viable in smaller situations. Waterproof rendering is usually applied to a brick, block or concrete shell and the surface can be trowelled perfectly smooth before painting it black. Black is the best choice as it absorbs light and makes it difficult to see the true depth of the water. Never use blue or, even worse, liners printed with imitation stones – they look foul.

Split-level water features

Features that use different levels and cascades need the water to be pumped from the lowest to the highest pool in the system. Most use submersible pumps, which come in a range of sizes to match the size and vertical height of the system. I leave my pumps running throughout the year, even in winter as this keeps the water moving and stops the pool freezing over. The power used is minimal and there is far less wear and tear on a pump when it does not have to stop and start on a regular basis.

One important fact to bear in mind is that the pool at the lowest point of the system should have a considerably greater volume than the top one. When the pump starts up water is drawn from the lowest pool to feed the rest of the feature, however complex this may be. When the pump is switched off, the water drains down to the lowest point. If the bottom pool is too small the water will flood over the edges and the system will need topping up when you get everything working again.

Right Rills are small-scale features rather like enclosed streams or canals that provide strong directional emphasis in a garden. They can either be left absolutely clean, standing out in sharp relief to the surrounding paving, or softened with generous planting, in this case a combination of *Achillea*, *Eryngium*, box and *Knautia macedonica*.

Closed water features

While open water is fine in many gardens, there is a whole range of what I call 'pump and sump' features. Even the smallest of gardens can find space for one of these. The most basic types are millstone bubble fountains, where a stone is positioned over a concealed tank and connected to a submersible pump. Water is drawn up by a pipe through the hole in the middle of the millstone, flows over the surface and returns to the tank below in a continuous cycle. The many variations on this theme include drilled stone boulders, glass tubes where you can see the water bubbling up and over the rims, glazed pots that work on the same principle and modern imaginative stainless-steel features. The latter can include spheres set in a carpet of glass beads, sculpted columns, serpentine walls, and bowls and dishes of all shapes and sizes.

Below There is always room for fun in the garden and this kettle pours endlessly into the bin and bowl. Construction is easy, with a submersible pump recycling water via a pipe behind the fence to the kettle.

All such features are irresistibly tactile, especially for children. They are also far safer than a sheet of open water because they can be set in a bed of cobbles, which are in turn placed over a strong steel mesh that spans the tank or sump below.

The sound of water is so attractive in a small garden and many water features are a real attraction for all kinds of wildlife. Site them carefully in relation to the overall garden design: water features often work best at the edge of a sitting area or close to French windows so that the sparkle and sound of the water form a focal point.

Wall-hung features work on much the same principle. A spout can send water tumbling either into a concealed sump covered with stones and surrounded by sculptural planting, or into a large bowl. A submersible pump drives the water through a pipe passing through the wall, up the rear face and then back through the wall, connecting into the spout, mask or whatever you have chosen.

As in all forms of garden design, the Japanese are masters of simplicity. In the traditional Japanese garden water 'flumes' are constructed from hollow bamboo, stoppered at one end and hinged onto a bamboo upright. Water slowly pours into the open end and eventually the device tips over onto a stone below. The water empties out, the flume returns and the whole process starts again.

Left This 'pump and sump' arrangement allows separate pipes to feed glass columns, some of which are filled with glass beads and set in a bed of a similar material. The pipe entering the bottom of each column will need to pass through a rubber seal at the base of the glass and the flow adjusted so that water wells rather than gushes over the tops.

Above In a precisely designed architectural garden all the features need to relate to one another and this water feature is a study in understatement. A sump set beneath the cube acts as a reservoir and the flow, via a submersible pump, is adjusted to form a gentle bubble rather than an ostentatious fountain. A touch of vibrancy is provided by the orange bowl, this being echoed by the *Crocosmia* seen in the foreground.

Ornamentation

Gardens can be starkly minimalist or brimming with all kinds of ornamentation. Neither approach is right or wrong, simply different and depends very much upon your personal preference. The choice of focal point or collection of objects is driven by the style of garden and the tastes of the owner. I very rarely choose these items for my clients, although I often suggest where a piece may go to enhance the overall picture. It makes sense that a pair of classical urns or period pots will sit comfortably on either side of a flight of steps or a doorway in a formal garden, while a striking modern sculpture might be perfect in an asymmetric or deconstructivist composition.

In some gardens things may not be so clear cut, but it can be a good idea to group 'families' of ornaments together, just as you would indoors. Terracotta, stone and

Left It is often difficult to choose the right container. A guideline is that it should blend with the overall style of the garden rather than fight against it. This tall silver cone boosts planting towards eye level and contains ivy and *Lotus berthelotii*.

Below There is a wonderful contrast between the stone balls of different sizes and the lanceolate leaves of the background *Crocosmia*. This is the kind of feature you simply 'happen' upon in a garden, set perhaps at the turn of a path.

timber are all natural materials while fibreglass, steel and glass fit comfortably into another group. I'm not saying you can never mix and match, but there is a definite affinity within the families.

In my own garden I have all kinds of 'found objects'. An old, twisted branch of oak I dragged down the field one winter nestles in a border alongside a path. I just like the shape; it has great movement and, for a piece of satisfying sculpture, cost nothing at all. Large, smooth boulders act as an occasional seat and help turn a path through a right angle, while an old milk churn, nearly rusted away in places, plays host to a sprawling mass of cheerful trailing nasturtiums all summer long. Beauty is in the eye of the beholder: if an old bucket grows a fine hosta, then so be it. You can spend a small fortune on pretentious nonsense, but I personally can't see the point.

Above I like individualism in a garden and if you can't do your own thing on your home patch, the world is a pretty poor place. There is no real meaning here, just a good sense of fun.

Right You can feel the warmth in the corner of this garden with its colourwashed and dragged timber wall. The old tractor seat is positioned haphazardly within the informal planting; its ploughing days may be over but life continues in an altogether more relaxed way.

Storage

It usually follows that the smaller a house, the smaller the garden. It is also a fact that the house never seems big enough to store all the paraphernalia that a family inevitably gathers around it. There is often enormous pressure on the outside room to accommodate tools, bikes, toys, plant pots, garden furniture when not in use, and much else. Space may also be needed for refuse bins, washing lines and that saviour of poor soil, a compost bin. In a small garden storage for all these items needs to be carefully considered at an early stage in the planning and integrated accordingly.

As I mentioned in the last chapter, it is possible to build a shed and site all kinds of other utility items behind some kind of screen or trellis to mask them from the rest of the garden. Mind you, I have seen many a shed to be proud of and well worth making a feature of. Choose a colour and let the kids paint it up – they will love it and it's far easier to clean up any mess outside. Provide some hard standing to park tools and wheelbarrows and dress this area up with a few large pots, perhaps for herbs or small fruit trees, so it doesn't look too utilitarian. Don't necessarily fit the building right back into a corner of your plot: the space behind may be just the place for a compost bin, while the side space could be turned into a neatly roofed lean-to for bikes, ladders and so on (remember you may need to make this area secure and/or weatherproof). It is worth remembering that a building situated tight on a boundary is almost impossible to maintain properly.

Climbers and other generous planting can complete the picture, softening the outline so it doesn't look out of place with the rest of the garden, even virtually hiding the area altogether.

Below Built-in seating can provide real potential for storage if the top is hinged for easy access. It could also be lined to make it waterproof. Such places are ideal for clearing toys and other impedimenta.

Above Beach hut, or garden shed with fence painted to match! Even the most mundane elements can contribute to the overall composition if you use a little imagination. Why do we turn our backs on such potential, relegating storage and utility areas to the most distant parts of the garden when we can so easily bring them right up front and make something good of them?

Right There is a good argument for making a feature out of a storage area and these shelves for flowerpots, topped with their little pediment and flanked by obelisks, have something of a classical air that is both practical and injects a little humour into the situation.

Play

Gardens are for everyone and outdoor play is one way to get children out of the house and into
fresh air. However, most mass-produced play equipment tends to be dire, only available in a range
of garish colours that children are supposed to like which stick out in the garden like a sore thumb.
A successful swing, slide or climbing frame should depend on its usability rather than its trendy

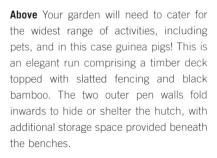

Above Your garden will need to cater for the widest range of activities, including pets, and in this case guinea pigs! This is an elegant run comprising a timber deck topped with slatted fencing and black bamboo. The two outer pen walls fold inwards to hide or shelter the hutch, with additional storage space provided beneath the benches.

colour scheme. As a child I had a stupendous swing dangling out of a tree; solid ropes bore the strain and Dad had carefully shaped the seat from a piece of beech to fit a young backside. It cost virtually nothing but was the envy of the neighbourhood. Not everyone has a big tree in a

Above In this garden corner a coloured bark mulch softens the landing area and the bamboo grove surrounding the feature doubles as a den.

Opposite While parents may feel this design may induce a migraine, the kids will love this – after all, the garden is for everyone! The colours are vibrant and fun and the floor pattern pulls the set-up together. Long may such innovative design thinking continue.

small garden but a solid construction of stout timbers can be screwed to a wall and extend out to form a play fort, climbing frame, support for a swing and toy store. There's nothing difficult about making such a feature and children can help with it. If you do feel the need to make it blend into the background, climbing plants can be trained up or along the supports, but don't attempt to try to grow anything too precious as the plants will come under assault from energetic children.

A good wall, preferably without windows, is another godsend for hitting and bouncing a ball against. There's no need to paint goal posts or stumps on them: kids make up their own rules and move around as the mood takes them.

There is an honesty about solid and well-constructed play equipment that sits comfortably in most gardens. It is a passing phase, at least before the grandchildren come along, and gardens are often designed and shaped around a time scale that allows such structures to change and be modified as years go by. Family gardens, thank goodness, are never too pristine or neat; they serve their purpose and serve it well.

Designing with light

Over the course of a year there are as many hours of darkness as there are daylight and a garden without some kind of illumination is likely to be underused. During the day we are naturally used to see everything lit from above or top lit. As night draws on there is huge potential for using bottom lighting, together with other techniques, to create entirely different effects.

As in any area of design, simplicity is all. A garish display can so easily wreck what is otherwise a sensitive composition, especially in a small garden. Lighting can be broadly broken down into practical and decorative effects. The former is just what it says, a way of illuminating doors, steps, paths and work areas. Where light fittings will be visible, say close to a doorway, then the choice should be in keeping with the overall style of the garden and adjoining architecture. There is little point in displaying a traditional coach lamp or, even worse, one of those pseudo–street lamps in a modern garden. Modern fittings go with modern design, traditional with traditional – this is simply common sense.

In most situations, however, it is the light that is important and not the fitting. The fittings might be neatly built into the sides of steps or placed at a low level so that they cast a beam or pool of light out across a path. There is little point in lighting the top of your head when going from one place to another. If you can see the fitting, choose something that is well designed. Remember that a light set among planting may need repositioning from time to time as the plants grow.

Be careful choosing the light-bulb colour. You need only two shades, white and blue, both of which tend to be neutral in most situations. Beware – all the other shades turn foliage, and most other things, the most revolting colours.

Some of the best lighting techniques have been borrowed from the theatre where creativity has always been important. In the garden I regularly use five of them to stunning effect, but don't overdo it: remember that less is inevitably more.

Below This is a pretty cool way to enter the garden, over a crisp band of small white cobbles framed neatly with neon strip lighting that in turn gives onto stylish black slate paving.

Spotlighting

This uses a tight beam to pick out an object in sharp relief. The source is usually concealed some way away and produces high drama when directed at a statue, focal point, feature plant or anything else special. Using a narrow beam means that the surrounding area is still in darkness, heightening the effect. But add spotlights sparingly, otherwise your eye will jump restlessly from place to place. In a small garden one or two are all you need.

Above Where you have a change of level lighting becomes particularly important, both in practical and decorative terms. Here lights are hung from above, echoing the waxy trumpets of the fragrant daturas, and neatly set alongside the steps to illuminate the way down.

Left Modern art and modern garden design deserve equally avant garde lighting techniques. This sculptural and solid timber screen is emphasized with vertical neon strips that decrease in height with distance. This increases a feeling of perspective, the whole arrangement rising out of a bed of lush planting that backs the curved seat.

Backlighting

Like spotlighting, the effect of backlighting is to pick out an object in sharp relief. In this technique the beam is positioned right behind the feature, producing a dramatic silhouette. Again, use backlighting equally carefully to avoid it becoming clichéd. A single well-chosen sculpture, or perhaps the tracery of a particularly fine plant, would be ideal for this treatment. In a tiny town garden I planted a single mature Japanese maple in front of a plain wall and placed a backlighter behind – it was perfect.

Floodlighting

This is the most simple form of lighting, using a relatively wide beam and low wattage bulb. It is often set at a higher level, perhaps on the house or in a tree, to wash over an area of planting, lawn or paving and provide soft illumination. The use of devastatingly powerful halogen lights is of little use in either decorative or practical terms. In fact very strong light sources create deep shadows where people become virtually invisible, doing little for security. It is far better, in security terms, to use a number of well-positioned floodlights that are easier on the eye and offer a broader spread of light.

Grazing

While the above are relatively straightforward techniques there are a few more worth thinking about. The first of these is grazing. Here one or a number of lights are placed as close as possible to the base of a wall, tree or other feature to cast beams upwards. This will have the effect of illuminating every surface detail or patina: the bark of a tree, the texture of brick or boards on the face of a building or the architectural mouldings of a façade.

Below With the trend for using old materials in new ways, the potential to construct all kinds of different garden features has soared. This Perspex bench has lights set inside to create a soft glow to illuminate the immediate area and highlight the sculptural planting above. The deck leads the eye towards the bench and is echoed in the vertical plane by the simple railings.

Right Lighting, when well and imaginatively used, spells high drama. Here all the surfaces are washed from a number of sources, the silver birch being uplit to draw attention to the pure white stems. This scheme is crisply contemporary with well detailed walls, paving and furniture, the lighting naturally emphasizing the fact and adding to the effect.

Moonlighting

This is a real favourite of mine, and romantic at that. Moonlighting involves hanging a number of relatively low wattage lamps high in a tree to cast beams and therefore shadows of the branches downwards. The effect relies on a plain surface of lawn or paving below where, on a still night, the exact pattern of the tree is picked out in a delicate tracery. With a gentle breeze the shadows dance, and, with a little music, so do you.

There are modifications on all of the techniques I have just explained, as well as some very hi-tech ones. Fibre optics are becoming increasingly popular for outdoor use and these can weave the most intricate patterns and pictures. Plasma spheres and lasers are possible, as are lines of coloured neon tubing that can produce high drama, as well as the occasional headache in the wrong situation.

This, of course, is the point. Lighting has such enormous potential to enhance the garden, but used insensitively will do quite the opposite.

Below Although it is usually the light rather than the fitting that is important, there are exceptions. There is a positive contrast in this eastern garden between the tropical planting and the oriental-style light.

Above Lighting water not only prevents an unexpected midnight dip but produces the most dramatic effects. Here soft pools of illumination glow from beneath the surface, echoed by the uplit bonsai at a higher level.

Left If you are going to show off an eclectic collection of lights, then don't be shy. There is nothing subtle about this but these hanging globes look like giant fireflies hovering above the path.

Bright light

While many yards can be dark or shady, needing materials to enhance what
light is available, quite a few will be just the opposite, with sun swinging across
the space throughout the day. I have never understood why so many houses
and garden walls in hot climates are painted white. This may look pristine but the glare can be
almost unbearable, particularly on a roof garden or balcony. The same applies to the huge range
of plastic garden furniture on sale – to eat your lunch at the table you need the darkest pair of
sunglasses available. The answer, as far as walls and other surfaces are concerned, is to tone things
down using pastel colours, cream or pale terracotta washes. These tend to absorb rather than
reflect light and are far easier on the eye. All these 'earthy' colours are warm and comfortable and
associate particularly well with planting, pots and furniture. These are colours that work equally well
inside the home, so can provide a link between the house and garden. Don't be afraid of using
colour in the garden. We use it to create all kinds of moods inside, so why should your outside
rooms be any different?

Above In the softer light of more temperate
climates, reflective surfaces can do much
to brighten an area. These curved stainless
steel plates set in pale gravel stand out in
sharp relief against the clipped box balls.

Services

Many things in a garden need electrical power, from lighting and water features to power points in a shed, or automatic roof lights in a greenhouse. It makes sense to work out the cable runs before paving or other surfaces are laid, as you don't want to excavate for them later. Wires are usually run in pipes or conduit to protect them from accidental damage. Power can vary from mains voltage down to systems that operate through a transformer; if you are in any doubt whatsoever, enlist professional help. Electricity in the open is potentially dangerous and an entirely different proposition to the supply used indoors. Fittings and cables need to be completely waterproofed and properly installed.

Irrigation

Irrigation is becoming increasingly popular in small gardens, which can be extra dry because of the 'rain shadows' of overhanging eaves and surrounding boundaries. In certain situations, such as roof gardens or balconies, plants will dry out far more quickly than at ground level.

But irrigation can be more of a hindrance than a help. I visited a garden where an automatic system simply pumped water onto new plants regardless of whether they needed it. The plants were literally drowning and the owners needed a little education to prevent the garden being killed with kindness. Plants, and young plants in particular, need enough water to establish a vigorous root system but no more, otherwise they will never be healthy.

Knowledgeable gardeners usually water with a hose, according to the weather conditions and the various species. In a small garden a hose neatly coiled away is a real asset. I have never had an irrigation system and probably never will, though I appreciate their value for people who are away a lot.

Take a good look at your garden, preferably when it is raining, and see which areas may not be getting water at all. This is something that you can do in the survey process mentioned on page 22. Much of it will be to do with the direction of the prevailing wind and position of surrounding buildings.

Irrigation systems can vary from fully computerized and professionally installed affairs to simple snap-together lines available from many garden centres. Some work with spray heads, others are simply a 'leaky pipe' that allows water to irrigate the immediate vicinity.

Right Light columns spring upwards from this soft planting like illuminated bamboo stems. This kind of effect is pure sculpture, underlining the inseparability of all aspects of the designed garden, both in day or night.

CASE STUDY

Seclusion in the city

If you want a clean, elegant and eminently liveable garden you will not get much better than this. It is the personification of the garden designer's skill set within a small city courtyard. But it was not always so and this space started life as a neglected yard dominated by a large, unattractive

sycamore tree. While such specimens can be wonderful where they have room to develop, they can be a pest in town as their heavy canopy casts deep shade and their roots drain moisture and nutrients from the ground. It had to go.

With the site cleared, the client's brief of a cool minimalist garden utilizing warm Mediterranean colours with an interesting floor and architectural planting could be realized. Although the Modern Movement flourished some seventy years ago, its design styles and ethos are as strong today as they ever were, being subtly updated by every generation of gifted designers. In this garden we have a sensitively worked asymmetric composition that uses a range of materials that complement one another perfectly.

Moving away from the house, a deck in Western red cedar leads us through the narrow passageway towards the garden. Punctuation is provided by the box balls in pots, and in order to widen the corridor visually the boards have been laid across the space, this same line naturally turning us into the main part of the yard. Here the view opens up, bringing the composition alive

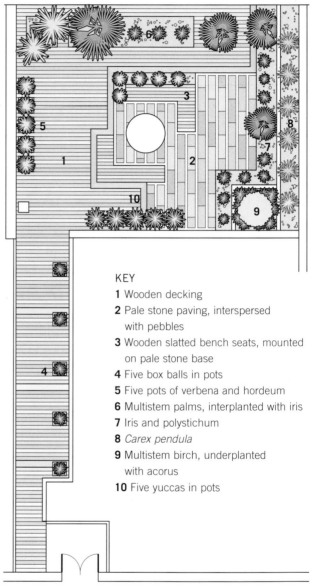

KEY

1 Wooden decking
2 Pale stone paving, interspersed
  with pebbles
3 Wooden slatted bench seats, mounted
  on pale stone base
4 Five box balls in pots
5 Five pots of verbena and hordeum
6 Multistem palms, interplanted with iris
7 Iris and polystichum
8 *Carex pendula*
9 Multistem birch, underplanted
  with acorus
10 Five yuccas in pots

Left Here many of the garden elements are drawn together in this secluded corner. Paving and seat base link the horizontal and vertical planes, while the inset blue panels introduce a dash of colour from the wall behind, the terracotta pots and yuccas adding a dash of counterpoint.

with a neat sitting area, planting and enough colour to brighten the dreariest winter's day. While the deck encourages movement, the sitting area slows things down with crisp courses of paving turned at right angles to the former, separated by bands of cobbles. Bench seating constructed from rendered and colourwashed walls, topped with matching cedar boards, contains the space. The blue-painted recessed panels provide a natural link with the main wall that provides a backdrop, the tall potted yuccas providing a delightfully sculptural counterpoint, the variegation standing out in sharp relief. The ochre-coloured walls that contain the sitting area bring warmth and help to tone down the glare of hot summer sun.

The planting of the garden is layered with raised beds, pots and ground covers combining to form an architectural but low-maintenance scheme. Containers provide interest and counterpoint, being used repetitively to provide a visual rhythm as you move around the space. Multi-stemmed birch, unlike sycamore, is perfect for a small garden, being offset by the striking palms that provide a middle layer of planting. At the lowest level grasses, ferns and iris, planted through cobbles, will develop into a carpet and the whole scheme will provide real interest throughout the year.

Above Gardens are not just daytime affairs and, in truth, most of us enjoy our leisure during the evening. This means that well-considered outdoor lighting is all-important and, as well as being practical, it can provide dramatic effects. Here the palms are uplit so that the spiky fronds stand out in sharp relief around the perimeter of the garden.

Above It is not always necessary to have pots standing out sharply against a background and the subtlety of ochre on ochre is attractive. Planting softens both elements and continues the repetitive theme around the garden.

Left There is a clever interplay of line and level here with the juxtaposition of raised beds and paving. Small loose cobbles provide continuity throughout, acting as a planting mulch that will reduce maintenance to a minimum.

Helter skelter

If you want a garden that rages against convention then here it is. Bold, busy, in your face, full of different conventions and materials. This is a garden that takes a sideways look at style, throws it up in the air and lets it fall, mostly into a preconceived pattern.

This is not a place for quiet contemplation but rather something to stir the senses and produce reaction – and a strong reaction at that. Like a piece of modern sculpture you will love it or hate it, but the reaction is important and is very much a part of what this space is about – pure art.

I always feel that interpretation for this kind of installation is very much in the eye of the beholder and

different people, including the artist, will see quite different patterns and symbolism. To me, although there are many elements here they are certainly not placed at random, there is a quite definite pattern that swirls out from the raised thyme mound and pivots towards the circular water feature in the middle of the garden. This produces a real feeling of rhythm and movement but is offset on the other side of the composition by the far more static, forty-five-degree angled low

Above Much of the fascination in this garden lies in the swirling patterns of different materials and here vertical slate fins swim though a narrowing sea.

Left Here the seeming Japanese overtones are very apparent, with carefully positioned rocks standing within the mounded shape of grasses against a background of gravel-like pumice.

Opposite Once you study the composition in its entirety for a while, the garden loses its seemingly confusing pattern and you can really start to see the inter-relationship of the various elements. There is a great deal of thought here that arranges the various elements into a strong whole.

Above Here the wonderful mirror wall really performs, with the hedges, planting, cobbles and pumice being reflected and distorted in an ever-changing pattern as you move past it.

concrete wall and the topiaried yew bushes. In other words two quite different styles are thrown together, forming visual turbulence, not unlike a heavy sea striking against a partly submerged rocky outcrop.

Although this is a thoroughly modern and exciting artwork, it seems to me that the real influence comes from Japan. All the classic elements are here: standing stones, clipped box balls and yew, the use of ground covers and grasses and, of course, sweeps of small-scale materials such as pumice, gravel and slate. What is different here is that the media have been mutated, the hedges are shaped into different planes, the rocks lean at ever-increasing angles and the use of modern and reflective surfaces are brought into play.

This is a busy garden – it is supposed to be – but the real beauty lies in the detail. Look closely and you will see the counterpoint of slate on glass, grass on pumice and concrete walls visually supporting clipped box. Here is excitement, ideas and above all fun, something that has been lost from much mainstream garden design.

To me, the core of the design is the curved, polished stainless steel wall that sets up fascinating and changing reflections as you walk past it. On one side the surface is convex, on the other concave (remember those fairground mirrors, were they flattering or not?). Perhaps this is the point, stimulation, memories, distortion, half reality – all these are things that make up our everyday lives, that they can be incorporated in a garden is refreshing. What do *you* think?

Right This view of the wall provides one of the most interesting aspects of the garden with crumpled panels of lead that slump off the vertical surface. It is as though the garden has tried to climb the wall, but has been repelled.

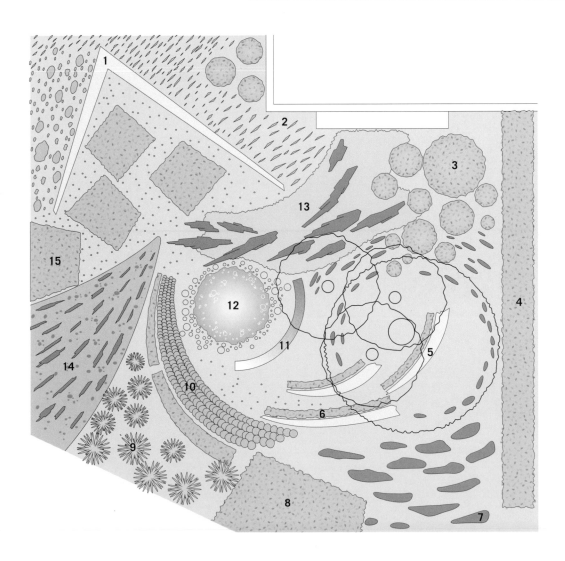

KEY
1 Low, angled concrete wall
2 Lead sculpture on wall
3 Yew balls
4 Hedge
5 Low concrete walls
6 Clipped box hedges
7 Standing stones
8 Clipped box hedges
9 *Festuca glauca*
10 Angled slates
11 Stainless steel wall
12 Water feature
13 Standing stones with drifts of grasses
14 Slates set in blue crushed glass
15 Clipped yew hedges

4

PLANTING

The importance of planned planting

To most people, plants are a garden and vice versa. They bring colour, interest and the softening influence of flower and foliage: in short, they bring the space alive.

However, the problem so often is that we tend to think of planting at the expense of everything else. We embark on random binges at the local garden centre or nursery, we get seduced by a glorious bloom, we watch a gardening programme and just have to have the plant the presenter extols at the time. It is no wonder that a garden can so easily end up a jumble of unrelated species, all fighting for space and pride of place. Not only does this usually mean high maintenance, but it is endlessly frustrating as nothing really relates to anything else.

Below Soft landscape provides a living mantle that brings the garden alive. Within this paved terrace, planting provides colour and interest, the delphiniums and sisyrinchium adding vertical emphasis.

Doing your homework

If you learn nothing else from this book it will be the simple fact that planning and planting is a sequential process. To design anything effectively needs a degree of skill but, more importantly, depends on taking your time, doing your homework and not getting seduced by the first pretty face that comes along.

There is a good deal of work to be carried out before you even think about planting and this is precisely what we have been looking at up to now. But you will still have been getting plenty of ideas about what appeals to you, and the more gardens you visit, the more magazines and books you read and the more you talk to like-minded people, the better your appreciation will be. Build up a file of the various plants and planting styles you find attractive; pin them up on a mood board, change them, add to them and learn about their individual characteristics and requirements.

By building up the overall garden style and pattern in the early stages of design, you will have naturally been creating beds and areas for planting. Your initial survey will have shown just how sun and shade swing across the space. You will have checked out the soil with a simple kit to see whether it was acid, alkaline or just neutral. You will know whether the soil is heavy or light. So you have already done much of the vital work not just to physically grow plants but to understand the nature of your garden and what will thrive in it.

Left Things can be tough on a balcony or roof as you are more at the mercy of the elements, but with the right choice of planting you can create a secluded and sheltered space. Here there is a wonderful synergy between the foreground grass, *Stipa arundinacea*, and the flowering phormium with birch, *Pittosporum* and *Olearia* providing background screening.

Planting style

The design of the garden may well dictate, at least in part, the species you plant and their arrangement. A formal composition may call for clipped hedges, carefully balanced trees and mirror-image beds of particular species. A freeform or asymmetric garden may suggest sweeps of planting to provide rhythm and movement to lead your eye from place to place; while the creation of a minimalist design needs thoughtful positioning of architectural species to add counterpoint and drama in a just few carefully chosen locations. The garden style, which reflects your own personality, will in turn drive the character of planting: crisp and chic, cool and relaxed; or perhaps the leafy fronds of a mini-jungle.

In the smallest of gardens planting space may be limited, which means that your choices need to be carefully thought out in order to achieve the best effect. Where walls are dominant, climbers play an important role in softening the garden and cocooning you within a less harsh environment.

Fragrance may be essential and so, too, will be the interplay of shapes, forms and textures that are such an important element in the creation of a successful scheme. Plants appeal to all the senses: sight, smell and, of course, sound, as a gentle breeze rustles through leaves or the stems of tall grasses.

Many people forget that even in the smallest spaces it is possible to marry practicality to decoration. There is absolutely no reason why you should not be able to grow vegetables and fruit in the borders, on the walls or in containers. Herbs, too, will add welcome fragrance and year-round colour to any garden.

Left Tropical plants often grow quickly and have dramatic foliage. These palms, with their tough foliage, need little irrigation as the coarse leaves transpire slowly, conserving moisture. The lesson here is to match your planting to the immediate environment or microclimate. As I have said before, go with the flow and resist seduction with unsuitable species.

The skill of planting design, at least initially, is understanding the principles of how schemes are put together. This applies anywhere in the world, from temperate English lowlands to the humid sub-tropics of Durban in South Africa. What I want to show you is the method that I use, along with many other designers, to plant a garden. There is nothing complicated about it; in fact, it is straightforward, underlining the point that simple things usually work best. Subtlety helps and the better plantsperson you become, the more complex and original your schemes will be. Accept the fact that you will never know every plant; there are just too many of them and nurserymen add new ones all the time, so don't worry on that score. Your knowledge will be directly related to your enthusiasm. Some people work, and I mean work, upwards of 12 hours a day in their garden and have an encyclopaedic recall of species, but most of us, and that includes me, don't. Never be put off by horticultural snobs who delight in rattling on about plant names ad infinitum; they are usually boring and their gardens reflect the fact. We all start with a little knowledge and, as the hobby grips us, we enjoy learning more. Being self-taught, at least in the early days, my pronunciation of Latin names was dubious to say the least, but as long as you know what you mean, that is all that matters.

Don't be frightened of plants and planting. It may initially seem like a huge subject to tackle and there may be an awful lot to choose from, but with a basic system at your fingertips the process will be both straightforward and fun.

Above There is something about looking out onto a lush composition that brings a feeling of well being, both for plants and people! This would seem to be a riot of flower and foliage although the area is carefully themed and planted. Trumpets of *Brugmansia* jostle with *Abutilon*, *Cantua buxifolia* and the fans of *Trachycarpus* to form a veritable but well-tended jungle.

Soil quality

Now wait a bit, it still isn't time to go to the nursery. There are a few things to consider before you do. The first of these is soil, which you will have come across in the garden already. Soil is the medium in which plants grow. Get it right and things will thrive; neglect it and things will die – it's as simple as that. The quality of soil varies enormously. In an old small garden that has been continuously worked over the years with very little added to maintain its fertility, the soil may be almost useless. What seems like ideal ground that is easily dug over may be nothing much more than sand, lacking in structure and nutrients. In a well-established garden, things will be different. While the ground may be equally easy to work it will have a far better structure and much greater fertility. There is no great secret to this apart from adding as much organic material as you can lay your hands on.

Organic materials

By organic material, I mean well-rotted compost or manure, as well as materials such as mushroom compost, used grow-bags or multi-purpose compost. All of these will not only boost fertility, they also give body and bind together a light, sandy soil and break up a heavy one.

Although people dislike heavy soils because they are hard to work, they tend to be inherently more fertile than light soils, as nutrients do not get washed out so easily. If you persevere with them, the hard graft of cultivation will be worth it in the long run. My own soil was pretty bad when I took over the garden but over the past ten years I have regularly dug organic material into it. What used to be a stony clay is now easily worked and very fertile, a joy to cultivate.

There are a number of organic fertilizers such as blood, fish and bone, pelleted chicken manure or bone meal, which come in packet form. Although these add nutrients, they do not improve soil structure. Inorganic fertilizers based on an ideal balance of the three main ingredients of nitrogen, potassium and phosphorus will quickly boost soil fertility but again will not help structure. With any packaged fertilizer it is imperative that you follow the instructions. Many people think that the stronger the application the better the results, but this will usually have the unwanted effect of scorching or even killing plants.

Left There is a certain softness about a well planted mixed border that inevitably appeals. Variations in height and texture paint a rich picture and here there is a subtle colour break between the pale purple *Verbena bonariensis* and the strong yellow *Achillea* 'Feverland'. Grasses have become rightly popular over the past few years and the choice of *Stipa calamagrostis* is a good one, the heads continually dancing in the wind to provide graceful movement within the border. Another ever useful species is the *Eryngium* with its steel blue flowers, this variety is *E. alpinum* 'Blue Star', a wonderfully architectural plant that adds a real dynamic element to the border.

Acid or alkaline

In your initial survey you will also have checked the acidity or alkalinity of the soil. This is known as the pH level. A neutral soil that can grow a wide range of plants has a pH of 7.0; acid soils have a lower number and alkaline or chalky soils a higher figure. Certain kinds of plants enjoy one soil or the other. Ericaceous species, including rhododendrons, azaleas, camellias, pieris and heathers, enjoy acid conditions while hibiscus, rosemary, cistus, brooms, dianthus and lavenders will thrive on shallow soils that contain chalk, which is strongly alkaline.

For some reason, the grass is always greener on the other side of the hill for keen gardeners. They always want to grow things that are unsuitable for the soil or conditions. You can create a specific soil mix in a raised bed but then the local tap water may have a different pH value. It will always be an uphill battle unless you have a water butt (rainwater is neutral) – something that all really dedicated gardeners possess. My advice is to go with the flow, plant what is suitable for your soil and let nature do the rest. There is no worse sight than a plant struggling for existence in unsuitable soil or conditions.

Considering the location

Your garden's location and microclimate can have a visible impact on what you can and cannot grow. Plants that thrive in a sheltered valley may perish a mile away on a windy hillside. Similarly, salt spray on the coast is a real killer and in the heart of a city pollution can be a problem. Luckily certain species are much more tolerant than others. Specific lists in plant encyclopaedias will tell you what to plant where – another reason for doing your homework.

There is a real problem these days that I lay right at the door of many of the large garden centres and nursery outlets. These often have a central distribution system that sends plants grown in one or two specific locations to points all over the country. So although you buy a plant locally it may have been grown in a very different area and in certain circumstances be quite unsuitable for your soil or microclimate. I feel that this sometimes verges on sharp practice, particularly if staff in a large garden centre have minimal horticultural knowledge. Using a truly local nursery, with staff who not only know what they are talking about but are dedicated too, cuts out the problem.

Local garden clubs or societies are places full of information and advice – one thing all gardeners have in common is their readiness to share knowledge. They organize lectures, arrange visits and hold shows. There is no better way to learn how to garden locally, and clubs often negotiate discounts at your local garden centre too.

Sun and shade

Shade-loving plants grow in shade, sun bathers in sun and if you have a wet or boggy place, there are species that thrive there too. Apart from a few real toughies, these

Right On a roof garden you often need to soften the immediate boundary but not exclude the view altogether. Hardy perennials, provided there is sufficient shelter and irrigation, are ideal in such a situation and here the mix of flower, foliage and delicate stems will provide interest all summer long. Species include *Verbena bonariensis*, *Melianthus major* and dahlias.

parameters will determine which plant thrives where. That is why it is a good idea to mark just what conditions affect which areas on your original garden plan. Remember that the sun swings higher in summer, with shorter shadows and that certain places, for instance in the lee of a high wall or under the eaves of a roof, may be particularly dry. Don't regard shade or a really hot border as a problem: there are plenty of species that are perfectly at home in either. Just be aware of the conditions your garden offers. Once you do this it will be easy enough to do some basic research and choose plants accordingly.

One word of advice about plant reference books and nursery catalogues. While these usually accurately describe species characteristics, they are less accurate on eventual size. The reason for this comes back to microclimate and soil conditions. A shrub that may grow to 2m (6ft) in one garden might only reach 1.5m (5ft) in an exposed position or as much as 2.5m (8ft) in a sheltered garden. Use reference books as a guide rather than the exact truth. Plant species are like people: they all look broadly similar but grow to very different proportions.

Above Town gardens are often shady places so you will need to choose plants accordingly. Shade is not always a problem as the soil often stays cool and moist, offering ideal growing conditions. Planting here includes that invasive little ground cover *Soleirolia soleirolii*, *Viburnum davidii*, *Fatsia japonica*, bamboo, ivy and ferns. All of these need little maintenance.

Indigenous planting

For far too long we have imported plants from countries other than our own, but now there is a worldwide interest in using indigenous or endemic species. The difference between indigenous and endemic is simple. Endemic species are native to a particular place while indigenous ones might be found in a country or wider area, but not everywhere within that general location.

In many parts of the world, lack of water is a problem and it makes sense to use local plants tolerant of such conditions – they will usually do far better than species brought in from elsewhere. There is also a danger that imported plants can become exceedingly invasive: many species that are fine in their home environment become vandals elsewhere. Many countries have positively banned plant imports and are culling incomers that have the ability to overrun indigenous species.

Some traditional gardeners are resistant to indigenous plants. They see them as uninteresting and frankly boring, but the truth is that there is often a wonderful subtlety and variation of leaf and flower colour that makes such species irresistible. They also thrive with much less attention than exotic imports and look entirely at home.

A question of scale

In a small garden the question of scale is an important one. If the space is say only 3–4m (10–13ft) square, a single shrub could fill it. On the other hand, this same garden could be handsomely furnished with a fascinating combination of smaller species for year-long interest.

Often the problem with plants is impulse buying or, even worse, accepting cast-offs from friends when you are not sure what the species is or how big it will grow. Resist seduction – something in a small pot, full of flower and gazing invitingly at you in a garden centre may be a monster in disguise. Always read the label. it tells you how big it gets, what soil conditions it likes, whether it tolerates sun and shade and much else. Most people forget this, buying the little dear and slotting it into a small gap. Two years later it has burst out of its allocated position, dominating everything around it. At this point you take out the shears and mutilate it so that it never looks the same again. I hate plants that have been hacked back. They never show their full beauty and in consequence have a poor relationship to anything planted nearby. I also have an aversion to the habit of neatly trimming every shrub into some kind of amorphous shape. This seems to be a plague of city suburbs, carried out by untrained gardeners to please insensitive owners – it does little for the aesthetics of the garden.

Left The real difference between tropical and temperate gardens lies not in the principles of planting design but speed of growth. Tropical gardens mature quickly but, if not maintained, soon become overgrown. In cooler temperate climates you can use the more delicate hardy perennials woven through more structural shrub planting but the overall composition will take longer to mature. The bright light of the tropics also means that strong vibrant colours get watered down whereas those same hues further away from the equator could well be overpowering.

Right Mondo grasses are wonderfully useful as ground covers and accent plants. There are many species within this family – *Ophiopogon planiscapus* 'Nigrescens' is almost black, here setting up a real dialogue with the pale cobbles and simple water bowl. Remember that a garden design need not always be complex to be successful; the simple things often work best.

Trees

Trees can be a big problem in a small garden. Because most of them grow relatively slowly we hardly notice the difference over the years until they dominate the whole garden – and possibly the neighbours' too. All too often this is due to planting the wrong species in the first place. Large forest trees are not suitable for small gardens and can present problems not just in visual terms but to foundations, drains and adjoining boundaries and walls. Some trees set seed remarkably easily; species like sycamore can be a monstrous problem in tiny urban yards with their heavy foliage and capacity to extract huge amounts of water and nutrients from the ground.

In many locations trees are protected by preservation orders, making it an offence to remove them without permission. Always consult your local council's tree officer before taking any kind of drastic action. Large mature trees can often be sympathetically thinned and lightened by a qualified tree surgeon. Experts know exactly what they are doing and you will avoid the unsightly and sometimes dangerous lopping often carried out by unskilled operatives.

On the other hand, if you are starting the garden or planting a tree from scratch then you can select a suitable species that will not grow too large. In temperate climates you will find plenty to choose from, including many species of *Sorbus*, birch, and *Malus*. All of these trees stay relatively compact and have an open foliage that allows light to penetrate to ground level.

If a neighbour's tree overhangs your garden this could be a definite asset in terms of borrowed landscape. A person is usually entitled by law to remove branches that encroach into their garden, but they should give them back to the owner. In many years of dealing with gardens I know there are more disputes over trees and boundaries than anything else. My advice is to be diplomatic and discuss the problem with your neighbour – it nearly always pays dividends.

Fast-growing conifer hedges that in truth are forest trees can be a problem if allowed to develop fully. If clipped severely from youth they can provide an excellent boundary, but even then are gross feeders, making it very difficult to establish any other plants close to them. Think very carefully before you plant them: other hedge species such as beech, yew or hornbeam are relatively fast to establish and need far less maintenance. If your neighbour has a conifer hedge, diplomacy is definitely the order of the day. If you share the cost of taking it out, it might benefit everyone concerned.

Below This really is the essence of a laid-back small country cottage garden in the height of spring, with fruit blossom over-sailing the wonderful lime-green *Euphorbia*. *Doronicums*, Solomon's seal, *Lunaria* and the neat ground-hugging *Muscari* with its cheerful blue flowers complete the picture.

Opposite Within a crisp and clean courtyard planting can be sparse and architectural, reflecting the general character of the area. Here the clean stems of *Paleo verde* stand out in sharp contrast to the purple boundary wall with spiky agaves punctuating the floor at a lower level.

Taking your cue from the architecture

Throughout this book I have emphasized the inseparability of interior and exterior space. Much of this is to do with the way in which you use materials and colour but plants can also have an invaluable contribution to play. We have seen that a formal design relies on a balanced approach with one feature and pattern echoing another. Planting will reinforce this and clipped shapes of, say, yew or box standing sentinel either side of a doorway or flight of steps will add punctuation and rhythm. In a Mediterranean courtyard, carefully positioned cypress trees will offer vertical emphasis, leading the eye upwards and encompassing the walls, while to some gardeners (but not me!) there is a definite fascination in the repetitive use of roses either side of the path leading to the front door of a traditional country cottage.

Where you have a modern house like that shown opposite, with a steel frame and walls of glass, the possibility of reflections comes into play and it is possible to achieve the effect of planting seemingly disappearing into the

Below The danger with a softly planted border is that it can become a mess, but subtle planning will produce the opposite. See the wonderful contrast between the tall grass *Stipa pulcherrima* and *Scabiosa* 'Chile Black'. That ever-useful climber *Humilus lupulus*, the common hop, clothes the house while *Acanthus mollis* stands sentinel at the turn of the building.

building by the mirror effect provided by the windows. Of course you can also take this literally by positioning plants both inside and out. Species with architectural forms often suit modern design and with these same glass walls there will be an almost seamless progression of space from inside to out. Aggressive architecture can be handled in two ways and while equally aggressive plant shapes, like those of the yucca, agave or phormium, will play along with the style, it can often be effective to reverse the effect by using a tumble of soft foliage that cascades over surfaces and blurs their outline.

Eclectic architecture where styles are mixed and merged offers the opportunity to have a similar approach in the garden. In all probability you chose the house for its quirkiness, so here is the place for those wonderful jumbled borders of hardy perennials that will jostle around the walls and then tempt you into the further reaches of the composition. Climbers will scramble over balconies and walls, foliage will tumble over steps and colour will weave its own intricate patterns.

Curvaceous forms and roofs are yet another possibility, the images being projected into the garden in sweeping geometric or freeform borders that set up positive rhythms as you move from area to area. Here will be the places for sweeps of single species, ground covers and lawns, interlaced with paths and paving.

You will also have noticed by now that I have a fondness for minimalism and simplicity, something that the Japanese have long practiced in their gardens. A modern or traditional building with a single twisted pine growing through gravel or a grove of bamboo wrapping around and extending the line of a deck may be all that is necessary, or a tea house set in a microcosmic forest or a stone lantern standing in a swathe of Mondo grasses. In a western garden a sublimely simple concrete block wall running out from a house of the same material, a platform projecting out and a great rough cast terracotta pot containing a mature cascading evergreen cistus, smothered with flower and standing out against the background, would be equally stunning.

Just occasionally, a garden may need no plants at all, but in most situations they are inseparable. House and planted garden should be as one, they both deserve it.

Above The superbly clean lines of this modern building are the perfect foil to the natural New Zealand landscape beyond. Here is a magnificent example of using indigenous planting, the great tree fern offering a sculptural background while the native *Carex* provides a simple but very effective low-level carpet of grass around the building.

How to evolve a planting philosophy

By now you should have started to see the advantages in planning a garden sequentially. You will have tailored your scheme around a specific set of requirements and parameters that will in turn have produced a composition that suits both you and the physical characteristics of the site.

Some people who are genuinely gifted with plants and planting design have an innate feeling for the way in which they can be positioned to achieve the best effect. They understand the juxtaposition of different heights, the subtleties of texture and form, and the interplay of different leaf shapes and flower colours. However instinctive this is, plantspeople are still working to a formula that forms the basis of a successful scheme.

As a professional designer I am interested in plants and have a genuine love for them, but my approach to planting, and that of most of my colleagues, is inevitably rather different. For the majority of the time, I am working on other people's gardens rather than my own. So I am more objective and analytical, and my selection of material is governed by my head rather than my heart. This does not mean that I am not creative or subtle in my choice of plants but garden designers have only one chance to get it right – hence we work to well-tried and tested formulae that we know will succeed under a range of given circumstances.

Taking this a step further, I will be thinking about the feel and characteristics of a planting scheme even at the

Left The British seem to have a talent for creating these glorious mixed borders. It is partly to do with the kind climate that allows such a wide range of material to be grown easily and partly an innate skill that seems inherent in certain plantspeople. This summer country-style border boasts a festive mix of largely hardy perennials that include lupins, *Knautia macedonica* and the great silver leaves of *Cynara cardunculus*, the cardoon. Poppies and roses rise above the border, the latter supported on frames.

survey stage of looking at a new garden. It will certainly not be specific at this stage but I will be noting the impact of a bad view or a prevailing wind and automatically deciding that these areas need screening. The garden may have a fine drift of existing shrubs or a bed of hardy perennials and while these may not be ideally positioned, they could form the basis of a planting that can be tied into the wider composition. One or more trees may suggest an area of woodland planting or drift of rougher grass naturalized with bulbs and wild flowers.

Although the preparation of a planting scheme follows on from the main layout design, it will be something that you are thinking about throughout the many stages of creating a garden.

Maintenance

When I plan a garden for a customer, I always ask whether they are a keen, average or lazy gardener. There is nothing rude about this enquiry: it focuses the mind on just how much work or time they are willing or able to undertake. Ask yourself the same question and be honest. Garden maintenance has a lot to do with how you plant various areas. To most people's surprise the general rule is the more you plant, within reason, the less work there will be. Plants that knit together will largely exclude weed growth. There is always work to do in any garden, usually peaking during spring, but with the right planting scheme you can tailor it to what you can manage.

Right This is a planting scheme full of contrasts and it is the combinations of leaf shapes that make it so effective. The great banana leaves of *Musa* overhang the pool planted with tall *Thalia dealbata,* with *Myriophyllum* carpeting the surface. Palms provide vertical emphasis while hardy perennials such as sedums and verbena add to the rich palette.

Planting in layers

When you create a garden you are creating a false environment, however natural it may appear. There is no such thing as a natural or wild garden; the space is, by its very nature, manipulated. However, plants are natural organisms and enjoy growing in certain conditions. This in turn is partly related to the type of soil, the proximity of sun or shade and the amount of moisture the area receives.

In a rich woodland habitat plants grow naturally in layers. Trees form the highest canopy, with native shrubs below and a rich carpet of ground-covering species at the lowest level. Added to this, there may be bulbs and wildflowers. In a woodland, space is not at a premium and although the overall impression may be of great beauty, the plants will inevitably be mixed up and something of a jumble. This is how nature operates, but a copy-cat scheme in a small garden would not be viable. However, the whole principle of layering is a sound one and you can apply it to build up a planting plan that will be perfect for virtually any situation, with trees at the top, shrubs and hardy perennials as the middle storey and ground-cover plants at the bottom.

A broad overview

As a designer I find this approach works well, but the secret to its success is to plan the planting in overall terms rather than a section at a time. If you opt for the latter, you may produce really worthwhile individual beds or borders but the chances are that they will not relate to one another and the overall composition will be disjointed as a result.

On your initial layout plan you will have designed the garden in overall terms – the paved areas, the shapes of the beds, the location of pathways, utility and play space. Do the same with the plants.

Trees

Trees might be needed to frame or screen a view, provide shelter, shade or just as a point of interest. Bearing in mind what I have on page 152, they should not be large forest species but something altogether lighter and suitable for the space involved. The smallest yard may just be too tiny for a tree at all, but most gardens somewhat larger than this may be able to accommodate one or more. Remember to consider a tree's eventual size, whether it is evergreen – which would be ideal for screening a bad view – and whether it has blossom

Below There is absolutely nothing wrong with growing collections of plants together but do take time to think about how one species relates to another and plant accordingly. This is a superb border with the great Saguaro cactus, *Carnegia gigantean*, rising above lower growing varieties that include *Lobivia* and the barrel-shaped *Echinocactus grusonii*.

corner of the garden: it will simply draw the eye and make the corner even more obvious. Better to use a group of a smaller species and drift these through the corner so that your eye is taken past the hard angle. I'll come back to this technique of drifting in a minute – it is an important aspect of planting design, creating rhythm and movement within the garden.

Another useful trick to remember is that plants with large leaves, say *Fatsia japonica* or, in a hot climate, *Philodendron*, tend to draw the eye and foreshorten space. Feathery, delicate foliage does just the opposite, refracting light and helping the view to recede. In terms of planting design, the lesson is a simple one: don't plant large-leaved plants against a boundary if you want to create a feeling of greater space; instead go for grasses, bamboo or shrubs with delicate foliage.

Security is a pertinent consideration and while a stout fence or boundary will achieve this, so too will a few carefully chosen shrubs. Those with spines or thorns are ideal; if they are evergreen, so much the better. *Pyracantha* is perfect, as are many *Berberis*. Both bear both flowers and berries and are attractive plants in their own right. While most of the bedding roses are too small to be much use, the shrubby species certainly are not. I have a hedge of *Rosa rugosa* 'Alba' I would defy any burglar to push through. Many large shrub roses with their vicious thorns are ideal – the flowers are a real bonus, many varieties blooming repeatedly throughout summer. Many mature shrubs are so dense as to be virtually impenetrable so their value on a boundary can be multi-facetted.

While background and screening plants tend to be shrubs because they retain their structure throughout the year, there are a number of statuesque hardy perennials that die down in the winter but grow rapidly in the spring and summer. Such plants offer counterpoint and interest at the back of a border and many a modest garden can accommodate them. I grow the giant Scotch thistle, *Onopordum acanthium*, in with shrubs and it looks terrific. I also have the huge leaves of *Gunnera manicata* set by themselves as a fantastic statement against the wall of a courtyard. Other herbaceous plants from the same stable include *Crambe cordifolia*, looking like a huge gypsophila, or *Macleaya cordata* with its attractive grey-green leaves. Most people with small gardens would never think of using such species, but they are absolutely fine if used judiciously and sparingly.

The middle storey

This is the most complex and fascinating layer of planting design and the area where the underlying design philosophy of the garden, in terms of style, can be brought to life and allowed to develop. Once the areas that need a specific background or screening with higher growing and denser material have been defined, it is time to look at the real 'meat' of the planting scheme. Here we shall be using plants that are somewhat lower, have greater inherent interest and are usually a mix of shrubs and herbaceous or hardy perennials. The palette may be rich or minimal but it is this part of the scheme that will really bring the garden alive. The rest of this chapter is devoted to showing you just what can be achieved.

Pattern and style

Those who have an eye for plants and planting design often tend to be flower arrangers, who appreciate how one form or pattern can work against another. I have worked with and learned a huge amount from professional flower arrangers over the years. Our skills are very closely related. You only have to look at the classic Japanese floral art of ikebana to see the synthesis of an architectural arrangement, or a classic composition in a chancel of a fine old church to see something in a far richer idiom. I am fond of minimalism and can appreciate the direct link between ikebana, Japanese gardens and Japanese architecture. The style of all these depends on purity and line, with a series of very simple shapes working in complete harmony. This is the key to good design: in no matter what field, purity and simplicity are everything.

Both garden and planting design are an art form. In creating a work of art, we inevitably create spatial relationships. By placing a splash of paint on a canvas, we give it a feeling of movement in a particular direction. Add further splashes and those shapes start to relate to one another. Planting design has as much to do with painting as it does with plants. The architectural idiom in which we plant can be lushly complex, with a wide range of forms working with one another to create either a rich and endlessly fascinating composition, or one that is gloriously simple. For example, the style that is considered to be utterly English relies on a delicious interweaving of species. Here you will find borders bursting with the most glorious, yet subtle combinations of old-fashioned roses, shrubs and hardy perennials. It is a complex and relatively labour-intensive style, but brilliant nevertheless.

In Germany after the Second World War a highly influential style of planting started to emerge, using drifts of grasses and hardy perennials. Landscape architects Jim Van Sweden and Wolfgang Oehme (see pages 78–81) took it to America with huge success and it has now returned to Europe, to be embraced enthusiastically by many modern designers. The style works well because of its relative simplicity and strength of purpose – there is no unnecessary fussiness, just the power of plants.

Minimalism has unfortunately not been associated with gardens in many parts of the world until comparatively recently, particularly those with lush growing climates. A Japanese maple in a glazed bowl set against a white wall will look as good in winter with its

Below These dusky deep colours smoulder and burn through the summer. These are mainly hardy perennials, but the overhanging *Miscanthus* and background of shrubs offer stability and year-round interest.

Right Planting design is all about the contrasts of shape and form. These cacti display these characteristics to the full with a wonderfully humorous dialogue between the ball-like *Echinocactus grusonii*, upright *Cereus* and the 'big eared cactus' *Opuntia*. Such plants are naturally site specific but if they are placed in the right environment ask for little in the way of maintenance.

tracery of branches, as it does in summer clothed in delicate foliage. In much the same way, a shimmering raised pool in California with a stand of cactus stabbing upwards in stark contrast, or a single pine, some four hundred years old, in a traditional Japanese garden, can be sublime.

In many gardens, however, the ideal will be to steer a middle course using our favourite plants, learning more as we go along and creating a scheme that is geared to the overall style of the place, plus a level of maintenance with which we are happy.

In the middle layer of planting we can play with the shape, form and texture of species; colour can be subtly graded and juxtaposed; and here lies the key to the overall feel of the garden.

Planting plans

When planning the planting of a garden in a measured way rather than working on impulse, it makes sense to prepare a drawing or planting plan. Professional garden designers do this on an overlay drawing, traced from the overall garden design plan, that shows the outline of the borders, raised beds and any other planted areas. This will be to scale so that we know exactly how much space we have to play with and can indicate the mature size of plants.

This is the first mistake that many people make; they badly underestimate just how big things grow and consequently over-plant the garden. A plant encyclopaedia or nursery catalogue will tell you the dimensions of an average fully grown specimen, both the spread and the height. Use circles to indicate this on the plan, the circles representing the eventual size. In this way we can accurately work out the number of plants needed in a drift or group and make a note of their height.

At this stage it is time to work out what goes where and how to relate those species to one another. A garden, even a tiny one, full of single specimen plants will look busy and restless. Your eye will jump from place to place and there will be little or no harmony. This is why many of the best planting schemes use drifts of plants rather than loners – although the latter can act as punctuation points (see pages 168–169).

Planting in drifts

This is just how nature organizes things. Wherever you are in the world, you rarely see plants growing in isolation. With trees you may see the seemingly endless continuity of an oak or pine forest; in South Africa you see huge drifts of wildflowers sliding over one another as if a giant had tipped great barrels of paint over the landscape. In the Costa Rican rainforests bromeliads and orchids run riot. All of these grow the way they do because they are suited to the soil and conditions. Not only are they at home, they also provide a feeling of permanence and rhythm, adding immeasurably to the landscape they clothe.

A small garden is not an expansive landscape, but it has the ability to provide the ideal home and growing medium for a wide range of plants. If you are a compulsive plantsperson, the temptation is to have one example of as many things as you can possibly cram in. Many gardens do just this, but they are not restful places. If you want a relaxing garden, as well as one that is easier to maintain, it makes sense to use this technique of drifts to the full.

If we look again at what happens in the natural landscape it also becomes clear that these groups or drifts of plants are not organized in regimented blocks but swirl around one another. If we use this principle in the garden, you can see how it immediately provides a real feeling of space and movement that will help detract from rectangular or static boundaries. In a large garden there is the opportunity to use large drifts but in a smaller space the numbers will necessarily be reduced.

The first step in building up these patterns is to establish the background and screening species, bearing in mind that the selection should take into account sun, shade or any other unusual conditions such as a strong prevailing wind or salt spray if the garden is near the coast. Shrubs will almost certainly be the best choice here, tough evergreens being ideal. Many of these are strong growers and in a small garden you may need only one or two in specific locations to achieve the necessary screening. In a shady place species such as *Ligustrum*, *Leycesteria*, *Aucuba* and *Garrya* would be ideal, while in sun you might think of using *Corylus*, *Sambucus*, shrub roses, *Berberis*, *Escallonia* or *Ceanothus*. Not all of the latter are evergreen but their dense branch structure will still provide effective screening during the winter. Here again will be the opportunity to do some practical homework by visiting established gardens before you plan your own

Right These are some of my favourite plants as they are so useful. The great heads of *Allium* climb over the ever useful *Eryngium bourgatii* and *Astrantia major* 'Roma' at the lowest level.

yard. You will quickly see how large specific species get. Botanic gardens are ideal in this respect as the plants should be clearly labelled.

Once you have selected the background, you can start on filling in the middle story of planting which will be a combination of smaller shrubs and the more delicate forms of hardy perennials. Throughout this book you will see a huge range of well planted borders that clearly show this technique and you will also see how this part of the border is the one with the greatest inherent interest as the groups overlap and contrast with one another. In a sunny border you might have several rosemaries and a single hibiscus, surrounded by artemesia, lavender and salvia, this being continued with a drift of the sculptural grass *Stipa gigantea* and the indispensable evergreen cistus.

The final and lowest layer will be the ground covers that bring the composition down to ground level. Here will be the largest drifts of all, and even in a small area you could be using dozens of a particular species. Such plants will also help to reduce maintenance dramatically.

Another trick that I often use is called 'cross linking' which involves using similar species on, say, either side of a path. You would not use these exactly opposite one another but rather in a staggered pattern that will help draw you down the path and help give the overall composition continuity.

The more space you have at your disposal, or the smaller the species you use, the greater the potential for increased variety. In a scree garden, which can occupy a relatively limited space using small alpine plants, you can build up a fascinating interplay of different species. Conversely, in a herbaceous border, which can still be quite easily planned into a small garden, the plants will be altogether larger and a similar number of species will occupy a correspondingly greater area.

Border profiles

If you take a cross section through a typical border, the general profile will be higher at the back and lowest at the front. In a double-sided border or island bed the profile will be triangular, higher in the middle and tapering down to either side. In the majority of instances this works just fine, but it can be fun to inject a little vertical variety by bringing the odd taller specimen into the centre of the bed, so that it rises above the planting around it. In a garden where low maintenance is a priority, this technique is ideal as the taller perennials, which tend to need staking, can gain support from the lower shrubby branches.

Shape, texture and form

This is where the skill of the plantsperson becomes evident and it is largely a skill born from experience. When you think about it, a plant, whether it be a shrub or hardy perennial, flowers only for a limited time each year. (Of course, there are exceptions to this and many roses are a good example.) This means that you should regard flowers as a bonus; for the rest of the year the plant will need to rely on its other characteristics – overall shape, the shape of its leaves and their size, colour and texture. To many of us colourful blooms are seductive, which is precisely why garden centres and nurseries display them where they make most impact and consequently sell more.

Commonsense, however, dictates that there is more to a plant than that: these other attributes will need to work hard when the blooms have faded.

In many ways I think this is where books about planting fall down, because it is difficult to show the overall size, shape and texture that a plant displays. The best way to see the real characteristics of any species is to go and look, really look. Go to good gardens – not necessarily famous ones – and take a notebook and camera. Notice what plant looks good with another and what the plant's real character is. Is the overall shape upright, weeping, spreading or horizontally tiered? Are the leaves ribbed, smooth, glossy, dull, pointed or palmate? How do these characteristics relate to what is growing around them. If the garden is open to the public, the plants may be labelled, which takes out a lot of the guesswork. Believe me, even as a professional of more than 30 years standing, I am always delighted when this is the case. Anyone who says that they know their plants is either a horticultural snob or lying – or quite possibly both.

When you start to understand what is going on, which is where flower arrangers have the advantage (see page 162), you will see that it makes sense

Left The secret to real success with your planting strategy often lies in the unusual or unexpected which in turn may require a little lateral thinking at the planning stage. Bamboos are extremely useful plants, having stems of many colours and when grown as a grove with a simple under-story of ferns or other ground covers can look just superb.

to contrast the rounded leaves of *Ligularia dentata* 'Desdemona' against the narrow blades of *Iris unguicularis*. Add the leaves of a Japanese cut-leaved maple above and the delicate flowers of a drift of white astilbes below, behind which rise the great leaves of *Rheum palmatum*. *Euphorbia characias* subsp. *wulfenii* could continue the group with their lime-green bracts while the glaucous leaves of *Hosta sieboldiana* var. *elegans* sweep below. All these would do fine in a cool border in a temperate climate. In hot sun the silver of artemisia could blend with the dark green evergreen leaves of a cistus, behind which the glorious foliage of *Vitis coignetiae* could clamber up and over a dry wall. Such bold foliage needs a break and rosemary would be ideal, perhaps in a fragrant sweep that leads on and down to purple-leaved sage.

These plants are not difficult to grow, nor is there any great skill in the arrangement, just a little knowledge built up by observation. I could fill the book with these sorts of combinations, but I'm not going to – it is far more fun finding out for yourself.

Above While the broad sweep of a garden appeals on one level and creates a good first impression, it will be the smaller details within that overall picture that are effective on another. Silver birch are ever-useful trees and the variety *Betula utilis* var. *jacquemontii* has particularly white, peeling papery stems that look wonderful throughout the entire year. Here a group of three has been under-planted with a simple sweep of herbaceous geraniums, providing a sensibly low-maintenance and low-key floor.

Reversal planting

Most good plantspeople tend to do reversal planting automatically but it is a technique worth thinking about. I had not really analyzed it in detail until a talented South African designer, Jo-Anne Hilliar, pointed it out to me. What it means, in essence, is that you do not place two similar kinds of plants together. In other words, there is little point in underplanting a variegated shrub with a drift of variegated ground cover. Equally, it is not a good idea to plant different species with a similar kind of foliage next to one another, because there is no contrast. Nor would it be very effective to place a pale or silver foliage plant against a pale background.

Instead, look for reversal so that variegation is paired with non-variegation, ribbed leaves against smooth or glossy ones, and leaves of different shapes and sizes. A pale plant looks fantastic set against a dark evergreen background, and so on. You can start to see how intelligent plant groupings, combinations and drifts are built up.

This theory is so simple it will work anywhere in the world. This same technique also works for flowers and I shall talk about colour on page 170. You do not want everything in the garden flowering at the same time. It may look fantastic for a month but not much good for the rest of the year. Neither do you want the same colours or types of blooms together, so the principles of reversal work here too.

Below The frustrating yet wonderful thing about plants is the sheer volume of them. We are always searching for and finding new varieties and ways in which they can be associated. This border boasts a terrific combination of colour, shape and texture with the dark-leafed *Cercis* 'Forest Pansy' and the pure white miniature flowers of *Crambe cordifolia*.

Punctuation planting

In any garden there is a call for drama, the ability to catch the eye and create a focal point. In terms of planting this is often achieved with dramatic or architectural species, usually with an upright or spiky habit. But a word of caution: too many of these will cause visual disruption as your eye leaps from place to place in an optical frenzy. Conifers, particularly the miniature varieties, are the death of many a garden if used in excess, as are shapes like yuccas, cordylines or phormium. Tree ferns have become something of a fashion of late, which is always dangerous for a species as they tend to be over-used.

There is nothing wrong with any of the plants I have mentioned, it is how you use them that is important. These are the stars, the prima donnas of the plant world

and like all prima donnas they prefer centre stage and do not want to be crowded. They are stand-alone plants that demand attention so anything around them needs to be in direct contrast. Upright spiky shapes love to be backed up with rounded outlines – the supporting cast that allows the star to be just that. Think of a pair of clipped yews in boxes either side of a doorway in a formal garden, a great clump of *Acanthus spinosus* against a wall or the architectural grace of a line of Italian cypress in an courtyard.

Alternatively, some plants really can stand alone: a cactus by a pool with a hot Californian sky above; or a steely blue fastigiate conifer underplanted with a dark green prostrate juniper on a bitter cold day with frost shimmering in a weak, watery sun. Both will look glorious but both are very, very carefully chosen and positioned.

Above Successful planting is much to do with scale, and the tiny green and cream lichens growing on this smooth boulder add immeasurably to this sculptural composition. Succulents enlarge the scale with their fleshy leaves, Agaves and Cycads occupying the higher levels and breaking the line of the boundary walls in the background.

Climbers

I have left climbers until now as they are exceptionally important in a small garden and also full of potential. Walls, fences, screens and boundaries of all kinds are not just physical divisions but provide vehicles for all kinds of scrambling and climbing plants.

As we have seen earlier, in a small garden the surface area of boundaries may be greater than the floor space, so to create a green envelope on the former makes perfect sense. I'm not going to provide a catalogue here, but there are number of things to think about, not least the way to support climbing plants.

Some climbing plants cling by themselves with little rootlets and these are best planted on a background that needs little or no attention: it is murder getting them off and almost impossible to put them back again. Others are extremely vigorous and would swamp a small garden in next to no time. Do some homework and go and look at mature climbers in an established garden to get an idea of their proportions and characteristics.

Many climbers are extremely fragrant. In a small space a fragrant climber can be positioned almost anywhere, but in a slightly larger space it makes sense to position one close to doors, windows or on overhead beams or an arbour where the scent can truly be appreciated. There is a climbing plant for any aspect or position: hot sun, deep shade, through a tree, over a structure or even as a ground cover – many species will happily ramble about at ground level before finding something vertical to climb.

Colour

I just bet you have been wondering why I have not mentioned colour yet. After all, it is what many garden owners clamour for. Well, colour is important, but it also needs to be understood and managed properly.

I'm now going to de-bunk a few things and the first is that ludicrous invention, the colour wheel. This device is utter nonsense; it has little to do with what happens in the real world, and by that I mean nature. It not only confuses people but also makes them afraid of using colour in the garden. (You can throw it away for interior colour scheming too.)

When you go into a landscape and look at nature, you will see colour mixed up completely at random. Nobody says that this is in bad taste or that nature should not do such a thing. I mentioned South Africa on page 164 – just see what colours get mixed up there. The reason it looks so good comes down to scale and quantity; drifts of colour are the secret.

However, colour is capable of a great deal and this is largely to do with the way in which we perceive space and distance and also the strength of light. It is a well-known fact that the hot colours, red, orange and yellow, are visually very attractive. They are dominant, drawing the eye and tending to foreshorten space. Position a great tub of bright red geraniums at the bottom of your small garden and your eye will instantly be riveted on it, forcing you to miss everything in between.

Above You don't have to reside in the tropics to create that atmosphere of lush steamy planting. Here is a wonderfully colourful and cosmopolitan jumble of species that include the bright leaves and flowers of Canna lilies, the ever-useful nasturtiums and fragrant *Nicotiana* planted in pots.

Right To achieve a single colour border takes a degree of skill but when planned properly, it can be decidedly effective. This border is a stunning combination of silver and white, the one enhancing the other. The shrub at the back of the border is *Buddleja alternifolia* 'Argentea', underplanted with *Achillea*, *Salvia argentea*, *Crambe maritima* and *Gypsophilia*.

Softer pastel colours, blue, pink, mauve and purple in all their shades, do the opposite. They are restful on the eye, they allow it to drift rather than rush and can draw your view out into the more muted colours of another part of the garden or, on a larger scale, the landscape itself.

So keep hot colours closer to the house, or major viewpoint, and allow them to drift into the pastels that take you on to the further parts of the garden.

Grey, silver and those delicious pale yellows and cream are the harmonizers that tie colour ranges together: they will tone down the vibrant extremes on one hand and enliven the cool pastels on the other.

White is technically not a colour at all, but it is useful for creating highlights, like a painter scratching off the colour on a painting. Drop it into a hot border to sharpen vibrancy and into a pastel range to give it an icy touch.

Above When we talk about colour we automatically think of flowers, but it is also worth remembering what a contribution leaf colours can make to a garden palette. Phormiums are particularly useful in this respect as they are evergreens and offer dynamic contrasts throughout the year.

Right Autumn, of course, brings its own charm with rich golds and yellows enriching the border. Here the statuesque stems and leaves of *Maclaeya cordata* contrast well with *Echinacea* and the grass, *Stipa gigantea*.

When you are creating a cool border, sometimes things can get a little too bland – it all goes a little wishy-washy and there is nothing to catch the eye. This is the time to inject just a splash of colour from the other side of the spectrum – a dab of yellow, a swirl of red. This will give the scheme a fillip, that merest dash of urgency that makes it all the more effective.

Planting design is pretty much like painting. If you are good with colour indoors then it usually follows you will be the same in the garden.

There are also sure fire, if sometimes a little obvious, colours that work well together and there is absolutely no harm in using these tried-and-tested combinations. Lime green and bronze – for instance *Acaena microphylla* planted under and around *Euphorbia polychroma* – or try yellow and blue, or purple and silver.

Now those designers who swear by colour wheel will be saying, well, those are complementary colours, or something to that effect. But good design is to do with what looks right and not following a slavish dictate. I plant yellow and pink together, which may sound awful, but it works fantastically in the right place.

Borders grow and develop, and need keeping an eye on most of the time if they are not going to get out of control. Like kids really. The secret is not to let things get out of hand, so that one colour dominates or a particular species gets a little unruly. Little and often is a good guide. This is the difference between architecture and gardens: one is dead, the other alive.

Above The deep, rich colours of autumn herald the end of the growing season and the onset of winter, but they are always effective at creating a late show of interest in a border. Here there is a delicious interplay between the dramatic forms of *Maclaeya cordata*, *Stipa gigantean* and *Echinacea purpurea*, all bathed in late summer sunshine.

Vegetables, herbs and fruit

In a big garden there is room for a dedicated area for vegetables and a well laid out potager can be a thing of considerable beauty. However, in a small space, it can make a lot of sense to plant edible items in the borders, treating them as annuals in the process. Many vegetables are extremely handsome: a cabbage, beetroot or globe artichoke can make a real contribution to the overall look of a border. They should be mixed in with an eye to their characteristics, like any other plant. Runner beans look stunning scrambling over a frame or obelisk with their fine red flowers and dangling pods, while marrows, courgettes or aubergines look fantastic growing on a bank where their flowers can be seen and appreciated. Cultivation requirements are the same as for any other plant; good soil being the key, with judicious feeding to get them really productive.

Salad crops like lettuce, carrots and radishes hold a real fascination for young children, especially the faster growing varieties – they are easy to cultivate and even easier to eat. As a child I can remember pulling them straight out of the ground and munching away – the soil simply gave them added crunch! This is one of the ways children become interested in gardening: it is a real hands-on experience.

Even crops like potatoes can be grown in a small garden. Just plant them in big containers (such as dustbins) that allow them a deep, cool root run.

Herbs are almost obligatory in any garden. Not only are they fragrant and good looking but they are essential for cooking. Fresh herbs taste immeasurably better than something bought from the shop and can be cut at a moment's notice. Many of them are Mediterranean and can be grown in tough conditions. I let mine self-seed all over the place: thyme, mint, marjoram and sage will all do this happily in the right conditions.

Fruit adds yet another dimension. Depending on what you grow, you may have spring blossom and edible delights later in the season. Fruit trees can provide structure within the garden and you can get a wide range grown on different rootstock. This determines how large they grow: a dwarf stock makes a small tree; a half standard is about right for most small gardens; while a full standard will probably be too big. Some fruit can be grown on small pyramidal trees that are happy in a container and others can be grown on walls as cordons or espaliers.

Bush fruit is another good option that doesn't require too much space. Currants of all types, gooseberries and, of course, succulent raspberries and strawberries can all be grown, the latter also doing well in containers.

Grape vines have been grown in courtyards since time immemorial and there are many good fruiting varieties that will even crop in cool temperate areas. They will create shade, colour and great clusters of grapes – what more could you want!

Left There is nothing to say that a vegetable garden need not be elegant. The smart name for this is a 'potager', but it's still a veggie garden to me! There are all kinds of good things here from espaliered fruit on the walls, tomatoes, the dynamic form of artichokes, the ever-handsome leaves of cabbages, mustard greens and the bright edible flowers of nasturtiums.

Right Fruit is not only good for us but can look remarkably elegant on the tree. These quinces are excellent for jam making as well as looking great set against the white wall of a city courtyard.

CASE STUDY
Wood and water

That gardens have their own character is undeniable, which in this case is a combination of the owners' needs and the designer's skill. It is also a fact that good or great gardens have a timeless appeal that allows them to feel comfortable wherever they are. In this delightful yard there is a cosmopolitan feel that would allow it to blend into virtually any setting, anywhere in the world. Indeed, this could be called the perfect small garden. All the necessary elements are here – generous doors that allow interior and exterior space to flow seamlessly together, boundaries that provide shelter and screening from the outside world and a wealth of planting to wrap everything in a soft mantle.

So what is it that makes this little space work so well and why does it engender such a welcoming atmosphere of comfort?

The secret, and this applies to every form of design, is the simplicity which is apparent in every facet of the composition. But because it is simple does not mean there is a lack of subtlety, quite the reverse in fact. This is a highly sophisticated piece of design work that embraces both the hardscape and the planting layout.

Most garden designs, and this is no exception, start with an interface with the building and this is achieved in such an unconscious way that one is hardly aware of moving from inside to out. This is reinforced by potted plants that occupy both spaces and the simple yet effective bamboo sunscreen that casts light shade but at the same time allows light to filter between the canes.

Left Although there are no curves in the underlying plan, the outline of the garden is softened by planting, reinforcing the principle that you need never be afraid of using architectural shapes. Here phormium, euphorbia, cordyline and astelia complement one another to embrace the pool that is covered with *Myriophyllum aquaticum*.

Opposite A garden should look good from every view point and I particularly like the vista back to the house past the trunk of the old apple tree. There is a delightful interplay of light and shade that is filtered through the lush foliage.

Below Stepping stones are lowered close to the water level so they seem to float across the surface. Moss softens the outline while that most useful of ferns, *Polystichum setiferum*, provides counterpoint in the copper-edged bed.

Left Sculpture can complement any garden but it has to look at home within the overall theme. Jungles suggest wildlife so these metal birds keeping an eye on proceedings look just right strutting their stuff through the ferns and ivy.

Opposite Come out to sit, dine, entertain and generally relax. This is what gardens are for and what good gardens are about. Nothing is left to chance with a carefully considered layout that includes decking, water, gravel and a well-thought-out planting scheme.

Surfaces such as decks have a natural warmth about them, encouraging bare feet and basking outside. Here the boards are laid across the garden to widen the space visually and as a result you are gently drawn towards the stepping stones that cross the small pool. Unusually this is planted with *Myriophyllum aquaticum* that forms a kind of watery carpet, another touch that is rather more subtle than open water alone.

Once across the pool, a broad easy-going step runs the full width of the deck and your eye is naturally drawn to the silver seat. This is another clever device and by introducing a dash of modernity with this bright reflective surface, the shady area is brought alive. This is sculpture as well as somewhere to sit and adds immeasurably to the overall composition.

The old apple tree is a classic example of not adopting that 'slash and burn' policy I talked about earlier. The leaning trunk and canopy sets the theme for the lush planting that brings a jungle feel to the garden, while also breaking the line of the well designed and detailed shed.

KEY
1 Shed
2 Gravel
3 *Fatsia japonica*
4 Mixed planting
5 Seat
6 Phormium
7 Cordyline
8 Grasses and agaves in pots
9 Deck
10 *Astelia chathamica* in pot
11 Honeysuckle
12 Pool
13 Laurel
14 Old apple tree
15 Background planting of laurel and yew

Planting does indeed bring everything to life with broad leaves and architectural foliage very much setting the theme. Flower is largely unnecessary here and the groupings of euphorbia and phormium, *Astelia chathamica* and cordyline, *Fatsia japonica* and spotted laurel all provide a solid but interesting background. These are under planted with ivy and ferns while honeysuckle and other climbers soften the boundaries.

The secret of this garden is a delightful understatement. It has also been created to a realistic budget, something that underlines its worth and long-lasting appeal.

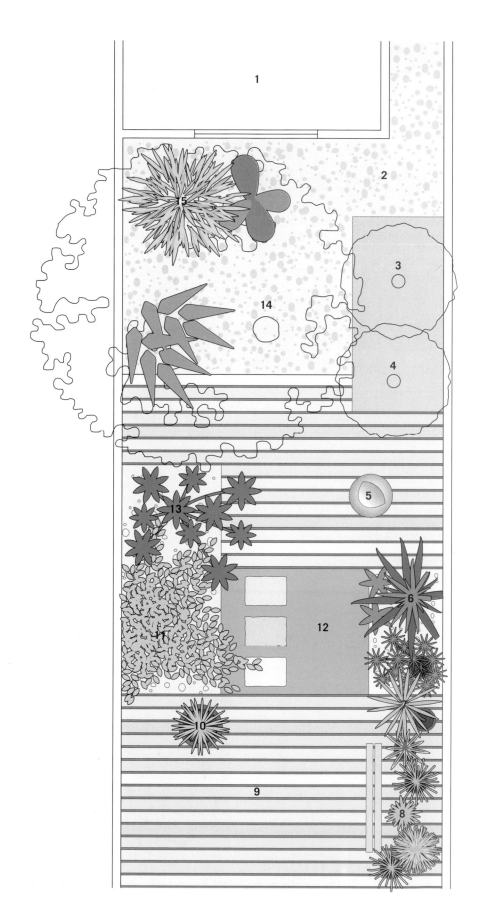

Plantsman's paradise

Gardening and garden design are two areas where there are almost certainly a good deal more gifted amateurs than professionals. Part of the reason for this is the simple fact that people often live with their gardens for many years and over that time gain a real insight into the characteristics of their home environment. This in turn may trigger a passionate interest in the subject and, just occasionally, an exceptionally talented gardener is born.

Anthony Goff was just such a person who started from a point of knowing little about his garden to becoming someone who simply cannot leave it alone. His passion and joy for this oasis is easy to see in the wealth of planting that has been woven and continues to be developed with a plantsman's eye.

Like so many, Anthony and his wife concentrated on improving their house for many years after moving in but there comes a time when you are happy with the inside and the outside becomes the centre of attention. If this is an uncompromising rectangle of scrappy turf some 30m (100ft) long and you have an eye for style – which the Goffs had already proven with their home – then the need becomes a pressing one.

They lived next door to the well-known English garden designer Christopher Masson and it was he who initially shaped the lawn and created the structural circular box hedge close to the house. This was a sound

Above Pots, in particular this splendid Cretan pithos, can add immeasurably to any composition. The real point with such a container is that it should remain unplanted, acting as a piece of sculpture set amongst flower and foliage.

Right Grasses have become immensely popular over the past few years and this striking species, *Imperata cylindrica* 'Rubra', is one of the best low-growing varieties, its vivid colour standing out in sharp relief against the neutral toned box. Above these sway the flower heads of *Knautia macedonica* with *Achillea filipendulina* 'Gold Plate' in the background.

Opposite In this view looking away from the house you can clearly see the architectural semicircles of clipped box that focus the main view out to the wider garden. The cubes of box contrast handsomely with the potted argyranthemums and the eye is drawn to the strong yellow of *Anthemis* 'Grallagh Gold'.

Top Some plants become a natural focal point in a garden and this superb specimen of *Hydrangea macrophylla* 'Taube' is just that. It is watered weekly with a 'blueing' powder to keep the colour vivid.

Left There could hardly be a better contrast than the glorious yucca in full flower and the statuesque trunk of *Dicksonia antarctica* topped by giant but delicate fronds.

Right Vine leaves cast dappled shade over the sitting and dining area that is elevated to catch a superb overview of the garden. The tall pots contain *Convolvulus cneorum* which loves dry sunny places while the circular table echoes the shape of the distant lawn.

approach as it offered an architectural entrance into the garden that then gives way to the softer lawn and ample room for burgeoning borders. At that time money was short so Anthony decided to undertake the planting himself over a period as time and funds permitted.

Knowledge was largely gleaned from books rather than garden visiting, which I find remarkable as it can be genuinely useful to see real plants in real situations. However, the approach has worked brilliantly but relies, at least in my opinion, on a genuine and gifted eye for detail and the ability to visualize just how large things grow and how they develop.

Of real worth is the rule that Anthony uses when buying plants, usually in groups of three species that look particularly well together. These in turn are related to the groups around them, providing a feeling of harmony and great continuity.

'Reversal' planting really comes into its own here with combinations like a powerful rounded box ball offset by the wonderful red stems of the Japanese blood grass, *Imperata cylindrica* 'Rubra' or the great leaves of *Bergenia ciliata* rubbing shoulders with the delicate flowers of *Geranium pratense* 'Plenum Violaceum'. Contrast is the stuff of this garden and yet there is nothing fussy or fainthearted here, rather a single-minded yet sensitive hand that is continually questing for yet another worthwhile and delicious combination. Long may it continue.

KEY

A Deck
B Table and chairs
C Steps
D Gravel
E Granite setts
F Pots
G Lawn
H Seat
I Compost bins
J Paved area
K Shed
L Path

PLANT LIST

This garden has more than 300 different plants. The 50 plants listed below are some of the most prominent or more unusual ones.

1 *Parthenocissus henryana*
2 *Vitis* 'Brant'
3 *Convolvulus cneorum*
4 *Argyranthemum frutescens*
5 *Taxus baccata*
6 *Buxus sempervirens*
7 *Ilex aquifolium* 'JC van Tol'
8 *Pittosporum tobira* 'Nanum'
9 Various clematis
10 *Dahlia* 'Bishop of Llandaff'
11 *Chaenomeles speciosa* 'Moerloosei'
12 *Achillea filipendulina* 'Gold Plate'
13 *Magnolia grandiflora*
14 *Imperata cylindrica* 'Rubra'
15 *Miscanthus sinensis* 'Zebrinus'
16 *Knautia macedonica*
17 Holly
18 *Myrsine africana*
19 *Allium hollandicum* 'Purple Sensation'
20 *Verbena bonariensis*
21 *Jasminum officinale*
22 *Erysimum asperum* 'Bowles' Mauve'
23 Pear tree
24 *Rosa* 'Guinée'
25 *Acer griseum*
26 *Beschorneria yuccoides*

27 *Weigela florida* 'Variegata Aurea'
28 Bamboo
29 *Alchemilla mollis*
30 *Rosa xanthina* 'Canary Bird'
31 *Pyracantha*
32 *Choisya ternata*
33 *Bergenia* 'Sunningdale'
34 *Fatsia japonica*
35 *Matteuccia struthiopteris*
36 *Dicksonia antarctica*
37 *Yucca* x *floribunda*
38 *Helleborus argutifolius*
39 *Geranium himalayense* 'Gravetye'
40 Various hostas
41 *Hydrangea macrophylla* 'Taube'
42 *Echium fastuosum*
43 *Angelica gigas*
44 *Cotoneaster salicifolius*
45 *Sambucus racemosa* 'Sutherland Gold'
46 *Acer palmatum* var. *dissectum*
47 *Ophiopogon planiscapus* 'Nigrescens'
48 *Pratia pedunculata*
49 *Lilium regale*
50 *Hydrangea quercifolia*

Resources

David Stevens
Well House
60 Well Street
Buckingham
Buckinghamshire
MK18 1EN
U.K.
011-44-1280-821097
gardens@david-stevens.co.uk
Provides international garden design, garden design correspondence course.

Associations and Societies

American Association of Botanic Gardens and Arboretum (AABGA)
100 West 10th Street
Suite 614
Wilmington, DE
19801
302-655-7100
www.aabga.org
Provides information about the collections found at botanical gardens and arboreta throughout the United States.

American Concrete Institute (ACI)
38800 Country Club Drive
P.O. Box 9094
Farmington Hills, MI
48333
248-848-3700
www.aci-int.net
Provides inspiration and information about concrete products and techniques.

American Horticulture Society (AHS)
7931 East Boulevard Drive
Alexandria, VA
22308
703-768-5700
www.ahs.org
Provides a wide range of horticultural information, including plant hardiness reports.

American Nurseryman and Landscape Association (ANLA)
1000 Vermont Avenue NW
Suite 300
Washington, D.C.
20005
202-789-2900
www.anla.org
Provides networking source for finding certified growers and purveyors of plants in your area.

American Society of Landscape
Architects (ASLA)
636 I Street, NW
Washington, D.C.
20001
202-898-2444
www.asla.org
Provides information to help you
locate licensed professional garden
designers in your area.

Associated Landscape Contractors
of America (ALCA)
150 Elden Street, Suite 270
Herndon, VA
20170
703-736-9666
www.alca.org
Provides networking source for
finding landscape contractors.

Association of Professional
Landscape Designers (APLD)
1924 North Second Street
Harrisburg, PA
17102
717-238-9780
www.apld.org
Provides networking source for
finding landscape designers.

United States Environmental
Protection Agency (EPA)
Ariel Rios Building
1200 Pennsylvania Avenue, NW
Mail Code 3213A
Washington, D.C.
20460
202-260-2090
www.epa.gov
Provides information about the
safety of various gardening products,
such as pesticide.

National Arborist Association (NAA)
3 Perimeter Road
Unit 1
Manchester, NH
03103
800-733-2622
603-314-5380
www.natlarb.com
Provides networking information
for locating a certified arborist in
your area.

National Garden Clubs, Inc. (NGC)
4401 Magnolia Avenue
St. Louis, MO
63110
314-776-7574
www.gardenclub.org
Provides networking information
about the garden clubs in your area.

National Gardening Association
1100 Dorset Street
South Burlington, VT
05403
802-863-5251
www.garden.org
Provides general information related
to gardening.

Netherlands Flower Bulb
Information Center
30 Midwood Street
Brooklyn, NY
11225
www.bulb.com
Provides information about
flower bulbs.

Perennial Plant Association
3383 Schirtzinger Road
Hilliard, OH
43026
614-771-8431
www.perennialplant.org
Provides information on the regional
suitability of specific plants as well
as where to acquire specific species.

Turfgrass Producers International (TPI)
1855-A Hicks Road
Rolling Meadows, IL
60008
800-405-8873
847-705-9898
www.lawninstitute.com
Provides information about various turf grasses.

Gardening Catalogs

Burpee
300 Park Avenue
Warminster, PA
18991
800-333-5808
www.burpee.com
Offers more than 300 types of vegetables and 500 varieties of flowers, plus fruit trees, shrubs, bulbs and garden accessories.

Gurney's Seed & Nursery
P.O. Box 4178
Greendale, IN
47025
513-354-1492
www.gurneys.com
Offers hardy, Northern-grown nursery stock (trees, shrubs, perennials, fruits and berries) plus vegetable seeds.

High Country Gardens
2902 Rufina Street
Santa Fe, NM
87507
800-925-9387
www.highcountrygardens.com
Carries plants for the arid climates of the western U.S., including winter-hardy perennials, water-thrifty wildflowers and native shrubs, cacti and succulents.

Jackson & Perkins
1 Rose Lane
Medford, OR
97501
877-322-2300
www.jacksonandperkins.com
Specializes in roses, but also carries a variety of flowers, trees, shrubs, ground coverings, bulbs, decorative garden gifts, tools, garden accessories and plant care products.

Park Seed
1 Parkton Avenue
Greenwood, SC
29647
800-213-0076
www.parkseed.com
Offers fruit and flower seeds as well as ground covers, shrubs and trees, and vines and climbers.

Seeds of Change
P.O. Box 15700
Santa Fe, NM
87506
888-762-7333
www.seedsofchange.com
Carries more than 600 varieties of organically grown seeds, including flowers, herbs, and vegetables.

Wayside Gardens
1 Garden Lane
Hodges, SC
29695
800-213-0379
www.waysidegardens.com
Offers hardy perennials, bulbs, ground covers, trees and shrubs, vines and climbers and supplies.

White Flower Farm
P.O. Box 50
Litchfield, CT
06759
800-503-9624
www.whiteflowerfarm.com
Carries annuals, perennials, shrubs, vines and bulbs.

Websites

Gardening Launch Pad
www.gardeninglaunchpad.com
With more than 4700 links
(95% of which are noncommercial),
this site has one of the largest
collections of gardening links
available on line, including those
to numerous plant societies.

Gardener's Supply Company
128 Intervale Road
Burlington, VT
05401
888-833-1412
802-660-3505
www.vg.com
Offers an extensive array of
gardening products, including
landscaping, pest control, tools,
composting, greenhouses and
sheds, plants and more.

MasterGardeners.com
c/o Garden Gateways, LLC
3701 Bank Street
Baltimore, MD
21224
www.mastergardeners.com
Provides links to Master Gardener
programs around the world.

Plant and Pest Diagnostic Laboratory Purdue University
915 West State Street
West Lafayette, IN
47907
765-494-7071
www.ppdl.purdue.edu
Provides information about animal
pests, insects and mites and
plant diseases.

WebGarden at Ohio State University
http://webgarden.osu.edu
This site hosts PlantFacts, an on-line
database that includes more than
20,000 plant fact sheets from more
than 55 universities and government
institutions.

Index

Acknowledgments

Conran Octopus would like to thank the following photographers and organizations for their kind permission to reproduce the photographs in this book

1 Nicola Browne (Designer: Ross Palmer, London); 2 Liz Eddison (Designer: Miriam Book/Chelsea Flower Show 2002); 3 Nicola Browne (Designer: Steve Martino, Arizona); 5 Helen Fickling (Architect: Pieter Mathew, Mathew Gerber Design, South Africa); 6 Mike Newling/Home Beautiful Magazine, Australia; 8 Helen Fickling (Michael Poyser & Paula Aamli/Designer: Amir Schlezinger of MyLandscapes, London); 10 Modeste Herwig (M Van Gerwen/Designer: M Pemmelaar-Groot, Holland); 10–11 Designer Jeff Mendoza (J. Mendoza Gardens Inc.); 12 Peter Anderson/The Garden Picture Library; 14 Nicola Browne (Designer: Steve Martino, Arizona); 15 above Modeste Herwig (Designer: P Janssen, Holland); 15 below Beatrice Pichon-Clarisse (Le Jardin Plume, 76, France); 16–17 Helen Fickling (Landscape Architect: Raymond Jungles, Florida); 18–19 Bruno Helbling; 21 Marianne Majerus (Designer: Julia Brett); 22 Marianne Majerus (Design: Gardens & Beyond); 28 Jerry Harpur (Designer: Bernard Hickie & Declan Buckley, Dublin); 30–33 Vivian Russell (Designer: Stephen Woodhams, London); 34–37 Rod Parry (Landscape Architect: Vladimir Sitta with Maren Parry, Terragram Pty Ltd, Australia); 38 Nicola Browne (Designer: Steve Martino, Arizona); 40 Gil Hanly (Designer: Rick Eckersley, Melbourne); 40–41 Nicola Browne (Designer: Ross Palmer, London); 41 Jerry Harpur (Designer: Ileana de Teran, Costa Rica); 42 Ian Smith/Acres Wild Garden Design; 43 Steven Gunther; 44 Paul Gosney/Stanic Harding Pty Ltd. Australia; 45 Henk Dijkman/Floriade 2002, Harlemmermeer; 46 Jerry Harpur (Designer: John Wheatman); 46–47 Kerstin Engstrand (I Lonnevik, Gammelkil, Sweden); 48 Jo Whitworth (Designer: Fabian Miskin); 49 Helen Fickling (Facer Hoffman Landscape Design International, Festival of Gardens, Westonbirt, Glos.); 52 Helen Fickling/The Interior Archive (Architect: Heinrich Kammeyer, South Africa); 53 Jerry Harpur (Designer: Dan Pearson); 54–55 Modeste Herwig (Ton van Bergen/Designer: Jos van de Lindeloof, Holland); 55 Marianne Majerus (Design: Gardens and Beyond); 56 Jerry Harpur (Designer: P Hobhouse); 57 above Derek St. Romaine (Designer: Cleve West); 57 below Marianne Majerus (Designer: Anthony Collett); 58 left Marianne Majerus (Designer: Joe Swift); 58 right Undine Prohl; 59 Helen Fickling (Designers: D Jenkins and S McClean, Florida); 60 Ray Main/Mainstream; 60–61 Jerry Harpur (F & V Vreeland, Rome); 61 Roger Foley (Designer: Gordon Riggle,Fairfax, VA, USA); 62 Nicola Browne (Designer: Andy Sturgeon); 63 Jerry Harpur (Designers: C Gaudette & E Tittlay, 'Catimini', Jardin de Metis 2002, Quebec, Canada); 64 Undine Prohl (Designer: Sasha Tarnopolsky, CA, USA); 65 above John Ellis (Designer: Andrew Virtue); 65 below Helen Fickling (Lena Tang/Designer: Paula Ryan); 66 above Jerry Harpur (Designer: B Thomas, Seattle, USA); 66 below Marion Brenner (Designer: Topher Delaney, USA); 67 Nicola Browne (Designer: Ross Palmer, London); 68 Helen Fickling (Designer: C Heatherington of CHDesigns); 69 above Helen Fickling (Lena Tang/Designer: Paula Ryan); 69 below Helen Fickling (Designer: P Garland. Chelsea Flower Show, Courseworks, RSPB/Severn Trent Water); 70 Deidi von Schaewen; 70–71 Clive Nichols/The Garden Picture Library; 71 Gary Rogers/The Garden Picture Library (The Carpet Garden Designer, M Miller, Chelsea Flower Show 2001); 72 Derek St. Romaine (John Naish, Brighton); 73 Marianne Majerus (Artist: David Thomas); 74 Modeste Herwig (Designer: Kees Ykema, Holland); 74–75 Helen Fickling (Designer: Martin Foster, Bark Garden Design, London); 75 Stellan Herner; 76–77 Claire de Virieu; 78–81 Roger Foley (Landscape Architects: Oehme, van Sweden & Associates, Inc., Washington DC, USA); 82–83 Michael Paul (Landscape Architect: Vladimir Sitta with Maren Parry, Terragram Pty Ltd, Australia); 84–85 Walter Glover (Landscape Architect: Vladimir Sitta with Maren Parry, Terragram Pty Ltd, Australia); 86 Helen Fickling; 88 left Marianne Majerus (Designer: Julie Toll); 88 right Clive Nichols (Designers: A Wear & M Melville, Chelsea Flower Show 2002); 89 Chris Pommer/Plant Architect Inc.,Toronto, Canada; 90 Nicola Browne (Designer: Steve Martino, Arizona); 90–91 Helen Fickling (Facer Hoffman Landscape Design, International Festival of Gardens, Westonbirt, Glos.); 91 Liz Eddison (Designer: Ali Ward, Gardeners World 2002); 92 Jerry Harpur (Designer: Topher Delaney, USA); 93 Jerry Harpur; 94 Matthew Benson; 94–95 Jo Whitworth (Bosvigo House, Cornwall); 96 Helen Fickling (Designer: Amir Schlezinger of MyLandscapes, London); 97 Henk Dijkman/Floriade 2002, Harlemmermeer; 98 Helen Fickling (Landscape Architect: Raymond Jungles, Florida/V Montifiore); 99 Modeste Herwig (Meneer Vermeer Gardens, Holland); 100 Nicola Browne (Designers: P Niez & A Schmidt, Paris); 100–101 Modeste Herwig (M. von Holstein/Designer: Paul Weijers, Holland); 101 Helen Fickling (Michael Poyser & Paula Aamli/Designer: Amir Schlezinger of MyLandscapes, London); 102 Helen Fickling (Designer: Catherine Heatherington of CHDesigns, London); 103 left Rob Whitworth (Hampton Court Flower Show 2002/Designer: 'Who Let the Dogs Out'); 103 right Helen Fickling (Designer: Martin Foster, Bark Garden Design, London); 105 above Nicola Browne (Designer: Mark Walker); 105 below E. Crichton/The Garden

Picture Library; 106 Clive Nichols (Designer: Claire Mee); 107 Jonelle Weaver; 108 left Fabio Lombrici/Vega MG; 108 right Undine Prohl; 109 left Sunniva Harte (Nancy Goldman, Portland, OR, USA); 109 right Nicola Browne (Avant Gardener, London); 110 Beatrice Pichon-Clarisse (Designer: Sylvie Devinat); 110–111 Eduardo Munoz/The Interior Archive (Architect: Sobejano Nieto); 112 Helen Fickling (Designers: A Cao & S Jerrom, Chaumont International Garden Festival, France); 112–113 Liz Eddison (Designer: Reg Wadie, Gardeners World 2002); 113 Helen Fickling; 114 Clive Nichols/The Garden Picture Library (Designer: James van Sweden, USA); 115 Ian Smith/Acres Wild Garden Design (Designer: Anne Swindell); 116 Sunniva Harte (Nancy Goldman, Portland, OR, USA); 116–117 Jo Whitworth (Chelsea Flower Show 2001 'Time for Reflection' Thames Valley Horticultural Society); 117 Helen Fickling (Nushimo Water Design/Garden Designer: Amir Schlezinger of MyLandscapes, London); 118 above Jo Whitworth (Hampton Court Flower Show, Designers: May & Watts); 118 below Ian Smith/Acres Wild Garden Design; 119 Sunniva Harte (Nancy Goldman, Portland, OR, USA); 120 left Marianne Majerus (Designer: Diana Yakeley, London); 120 right Jerry Harpur (Designer: Paul Smith, Jardin de Metis 2002, Quebec, Canada); 121 Andreas von Finsiedel/Red Cover; 122 Nicola Browne (Designer: Topher Delaney); 123 left Marianne Majerus (Designer: Diana Yakeley, London); 123 right Liz Eddison; 124 Clive Nichols (Designer: Stephen Woodhams, London); 124–125 John Glover/The Garden Picture Library (Chelsea Flower Show 2001/Designers: Cleve West and Johnny Woodford); 125 Jerry Harpur (Getty Garden, San Francisco/Designer: Topher Delaney, USA); 126 Ray Main/Mainstream; 126–127 Peter Clarke/Light on Landscape ITV Ltd Australia/Duologion Jack Merlo, Melbourne, Australia); 128 Jerry Harpur (Designer: Made Wijaya, Bali); 128–129 John Ellis; 129 Liz Eddison (Chelsea Flower Show 2000/ Design:spidergarden.com); 130 Helen Fickling (Designer: Tony Heywood, Conceptual Gardens, International Festival of Gardens, Westonbirt, Glos.); 131 Clive Nichols/The Garden Picture Library (Hampton Court Flower Show 1997/Designer: Barbara Hunt, Natural and Oriental Water Garden); 132–135 Helen Fickling (Olivia Bernard/Designer: Amir Schlezinger of MyLandscapes); 136–139 Clive Nichols (Designer: Tony Heywood, Conceptual Gardens, London); 140 Marianne Majerus (Design: Gardens and Beyond); 142 Liz Eddison (Whichford Pottery); 143 Marianne Majerus (Designer: Declan Buckley); 144 Jerry Harpur (Mr Wee, Singapore); 145 Clive Nichols/The Garden Picture Library (Designer: Sonny Garcia, San Francisco); 146–147 Marianne Majerus (Designer: Lee Heykoop); 148 Nicola Browne (Designer: Jinny Blom); 149 Marianne Majerus (Designer: Declan Buckley); 150 Helen Fickling (Landscape Architect: Raymond Jungles, Florida); 151 Mike Newling/Home Beautiful Magazine, Australia; 152 Marcus Harpur (Eastgrove Cottage, Worcestershire); 152–153 Nicola Browne (Designer: Steve Martino, Arizona, USA); 154 Beatrice Pichon-Clarisse (Le Jardin Plume, 76, France); 155 Nicola Browne (Designer: Ted Smyth, New Zealand); 156 Jerry Harpur (Helmingham Hall, Suffolk); 157 Marcus Harpur (Paul Spraklin, Essex); 158 Zara McCalmont/The Garden Picture Library; 159 Jerry Harpur (Agneta Sjostedt, Stockholm/Designer: Ulf Nordfjell, Sweden); 160 Marianne Majerus (Designer: Declan Buckley); 162 Clive Nichols (Swinton Lane, Worcester); 163 Jerry Harpur (D Gabouard/Villa Florin); 164–165 Marcus Harpur (Designer: Piet Oudolf, RHS Wisley, Surrey); 166 Helen Fickling; 167 Jo Whitworth (Alan Titchmarch, Barleywood); 168 Jerry Harpur; 169 Michael Paul (Designer: Rod Barnett, Auckland, New Zealand); 170 Saxon Holt; 171 Francois de Heel/The Garden Picture Library; 172 above Anne Green-Armytage; 172 below Mark Bolton/The Garden Picture Library; 173 Anne Green-Armytage (Sun House, Long Melford, Suffolk); 174 Jerry Pavia; 175 Helen Fickling (Designer: Martin Foster, Bark Garden Design, London); 176–178 Derek St. Romaine (Mr & Mrs Coelho/Designer: Cleve West, London/Seat design: Finn Stone for Modern Garden Company); 180–182 Vivian Russell (Designer: Anthony Goff, London); 184 Nicola Browne (Designer: Steve Martino, Arizona, USA); 186 Michael Paul (Designer: Rod Barnett, Auckland, New Zealand)

Every effort has been made to trace the copyright holders. We apologize in advance for any unintentional omission, and would be pleased to insert the appropriate acknowledgments in any subsequent edition

The author and publishers would also like to thank the garden designers and owners who allowed us to photograph their gardens for the case studies.

Author's Acknowledgments

Simply writing a book is just the tip of an iceberg; there is a whole load of other dedicated people apart from the author!

Special thanks to my two editors, Muna Reyal and Gillian Haslam, who have toiled with my grammar and split infinitives, Mel Watson, one of the best picture researchers and good people around, and Alison Fenton who was responsible for the all-important creative layout of the book. At the beginning we were simply acquaintances, we are now good friends.